The Pas

C000083089

As It Actually Happened

by D. Michael Cotten

ISBN# 978-1-936497-19-5

Scripture citations in the footnotes are from
The Complete Jewish Bible.

Searchlight Press
Who are you looking for?
Publishers of thoughtful Christian books since
1994.
5634 Ledgestone Drive
Dallas, Texas 75214
888.896.6081
info@Searchlight-Press.com
www.Searchlight-Press.com

Introduction

Luke 24:44 Then He said to them, "These are the words which I spoke to you while I was still with you, that all things must be fulfilled which were written in the Law of Moses and the Prophets and the Psalms concerning Me." <u>And He opened their understanding, that they might comprehend the Scriptures.</u> Then He said to them, "<u>Thus it is written, and thus it was necessary</u> for the Christ to suffer and to rise from the dead the third day, and that repentance and remission of sins should be preached in His name to all nations, beginning at Jerusalem. And you are witnesses of these things. Behold, I send the Promise of My Father upon you; but tarry in the city of Jerusalem until you are endued with power from on high." And He led them out as far as Bethany, and He lifted up His hands and blessed them.

Jesus Christ, the evening after his resurrection, declared to his disciples **"the inerrancy" of GOD's Word** and said, " all things must be fulfilled which were written in the Law of Moses, the Prophets, and the Psalms concerning Me."… And "Thus it is written, and thus it was necessary for The Christ to suffer and to rise from the dead the third day" Luke 24:36-44. **The unbreakable promises of GOD form the foundation for our faith and Jesus Christ is announcing, to His Disciples, that we can count on God's Word and all its Promises.**

These words spoken to us by our LORD leave no room for compromise or conjecture, **HIS life must answer the demands of the Old Testament in every detail, nuance, date, and implied picture.** Father GOD inspired the written word and revealed it to us by our LORD Jesus

Christ. As believers, now indwelt by the HOLY SPIRIT we have GOD with us to open our understanding that we might comprehend the scriptures, both Old and New Testament. Upon this foundation we can love our GOD with all our heart and our neighbor as ourselves, for it is in service that GOD's love is perfected.

Table of Contents

**Our Faith relies on The Unbreakable Promises of
Our GOD.**

Chapter One

**The life of Jesus Christ is divinely orchestrated
to fulfill each and every
requirement of Scripture and Prophesy.**

The following chapters are a comparison of the Christian
celebration of Easter contrasted to the Passion Week
Celebration of the Spring Feasts of GOD, Passover,
Unleavened Bread, and First Fruits.

Jesus Christ fulfillment of each part of the Feasts of GOD
gives us an even deeper understanding of GOD's love for
us and the incredible sacrifice of His Son Jesus Christ. No
doctrines will be changed, but understanding of the week
of the Lord's "Passion" will be increased and even more
beauty will be added to Passover season when we observe
GOD's unbreakable promises and their fulfillment.

Jesus Christ was a Jew, his disciples were Jewish, he was
preaching to the Jews, the great commission was given to
the Jews, almost all of the healings were to Jews, Jesus
celebrated the Feasts of GOD set up for the Jews, the word
Christian did not start until fifteen years after Jesus was
resurrected. Jesus did not celebrate Easter he celebrated
Passover, Unleavened Bread, and First Fruits, as Christians
we need to look at the Passion Week from a foundation of
the Spring Feasts of GOD.

**The Matrix of life during the Passion week
includes different Peoples, Nations and Cultures.**

1. <u>Culture</u>

Participation in The Feasts of GOD was not an option for the Jews, the feasts were not to honor Abraham, or Noah, or Elijah, or Peter, or Paul, they were not to honor ISRAEL or the battles fought, or wars won, or temples built, or entering the Promised land. They were GOD's appointed times for HIM to fellowship with his people. These feasts were to remember GOD's deliverance of Israel from slavery, GOD's provision for Israel in the desert, and GOD's promise of the lamb to Abraham and they were to be celebrated forever.

2. <u>Constituents</u>

The High Priest and Sanhedrin were afraid for their way of life and Nation. Listen to the description of the Hebrew leadership in the Gospel of John.

> John 11:45 Then many of the Jews (Pharisees who had come to mourn Lazarus death) who had come to Mary, and had seen the things Jesus did, believed in Him. But some of them went away to the Pharisees and told them the things Jesus did. Then the chief priests and the Pharisees gathered a council and said, "What shall we do? For this Man works many signs. If we let Him alone like this, **everyone will believe in Him, and the Romans will come and take away both our place and nation."**

3. The overriding concern for the Jewish people was the fear of causing GOD's disfavor by not obeying all the man-made additions to the Torah. Also, Fear that the High Priest would do something that would defile himself and the nation and restrict GOD's blessing from falling on the Hebrew Nation and their crops. It appears that the Jews believed that the rain for their crops was in GOD's favor and if they did everything required of the Jewish Nation they then had earned the rain by their rituals and sacrifices.

4. The overriding hope of the Jewish people was that The Messiah would come this Passover and deliver them from the Roman occupiers similar to Israel's deliverance from Egyptian slavery.

5. The Romans were great conquerors and Nation builders, they built new roads and aqueducts and buildings using conquered labor and then charged the conquered to use them. The references to the hated tax collectors were men, many in the Jewish community, whose job was charging for walking on the roads or drawing water, etc.

6. GOD had chosen Himself a lamb:
> to finish transgression,
> to put an end to sin,
> to atone for wickedness,
> to bring in everlasting righteousness,
> to anoint the most holy. Daniel 9
> To usher in GOD's new covenant, with its new High Priest, and to begin the Church, that whosoever believeth in Jesus Christ shall not

perish but have everlasting life.

Putting together all these facets of life in Jerusalem in the years of the ministry of Jesus Christ, we are ready to investigate "The Passion" of our Christ.

GOD loves us and his plan is established and "His Word" lines up with incredible specificity to set out dates, demands, and fulfillments on the life of Jesus Christ. There are more than three hundred fulfilled prophesies on the first coming of the Lord.

Jesus fulfilled the need for blood sacrifices required in the spring Feasts of the Lord, the shadow picture of the Jewish wedding, and the requirements of the Torah, Psalms, and Prophets. In HIM, who is our Savior and GOD, not some, but all, the Torah has been fulfilled by our Lord Jesus Christ for his "first coming".

Prophetic demands on the Life and Ministry of Jesus Christ from the Old Testament

Listed below are seventeen of over three hundred Prophecies fulfilled about the "first coming" of Jesus Christ, the Messiah. These scriptures are part of the most well-known prophetic demands about the life, death and resurrection of our Savior. They provide irrefutable evidence for the inspiration of Scripture, clear reasons to trust in the message of Scripture, and a grounded faith in the consummation of God's plan for the ages.

1. Messiah to be born in Bethlehem
   Micah 5:2, fulfilled   Matt. 2:1-6, Luke 2:1-20
2. Messiah was to be born of a virgin
   Isaiah 7:14, fulfilled   Matt 1:18-25, Luke 1:26-38
3. Messiah, prophet like unto Moses
   Deut. 18:15 18:19, fulfilled John 7:40
4. Messiah, enter Jerusalem in Triumph
   Zech 9:9, fulfilled Matt. 21:1-9, John 12:12-16
5. Messiah, rejected by his own people
   Isaiah 53:1, fulfilled Matt. 26:3-4; John 12:37-43
   Psalm 118:22, fulfilled Acts 4:1-12
6. Messiah betrayed by one follower
   Psalm 41:9, fulfilled Matt 26:14-16, 47-50; Luke 22:19-23
7. Messiah to be tried and condemned
   Isaiah 53:8, fulfilled Luke 23:1-25; Matt 27:1-2
8. Messiah, silent before his accusers
   Isaiah 53:7, fulfilled Matt 27:12-14; Mark 15:3-4; Luke 23:8-10
9. Messiah struck and spat on by enemies
   Isaiah 50:6, fulfilled Matt 26:67, 27:30; Mark 14:65
10. Messiah mocked and insulted
    Psalm 22:7-8, fulfilled Matt 27:39-44; Luke 23:11,35
11. Messiah to die by crucifixion
    Psalm 22:14,16, fulfilled Matt 27:31; Mark 15:20,25
12. Messiah to suffer with criminals
    Isaiah 53:12, fulfilled Matt 27:38; Mark 15:27-28

13. Messiah's garments ownership
    Psalm 22:18, fulfilled Matthew 27:35; chosen by casting lots John 19:23-24
14. Messiah's bones not to be broken
    Exodus 12:46, fulfilled John 19:31-36
15. Messiah given vinegar for thirst
    Psalm 69:21, fulfilled Matt 27:34; John 19:28-30
16. Messiah to die as sacrifice for sin
    Isaiah 53:5-6, 8, 10-12, fulfilled John 1:29, 11:49-52 Acts 10:43, 13:38-39 fulfilled
17. Messiah to be raised from the dead
    Psalm 16:10, fulfilled Acts 2:22-32; Matt 28:1-10

It is amazing that these prophetic references were all fulfilled, but it is MORE amazing that there are **no prophetic references to the Lord's first coming that were not fulfilled.**

**Abraham obeyed the voice of the LORD
And The LORD gave Abraham's seed
The Promise of the Messiah.**

Prophesy of GOD providing HIMSELF a Lamb.

Gen 22:4 Then on the third day Abraham lifted his eyes and saw the place afar off. And Abraham said to his young men, "Stay here with the donkey; the lad and I will go yonder and worship, and we will come back to you." So Abraham took the wood of the burnt offering and laid it on Isaac his son; and he took the fire in his hand, and a knife, and the two of them went together. But Isaac spoke to

Abraham his father and said, "My father!" And he said, "Here I am, my son." Then he said, **"Look, the fire and the wood, but where is the lamb for a burnt offering?" And Abraham said, "My son, God will provide for Himself the lamb for a burnt offering."** So the two of them went together. Then they came to the place of which God had told him. And Abraham built an altar there and placed the wood in order; and **he bound Isaac his son and laid him on the altar, upon the wood. And Abraham stretched out his hand and took the knife to slay his son.**

But the Angel of the LORD called to him from heaven and said, "Abraham, Abraham!" So he said, "Here I am." And He said, **"Do not lay your hand on the lad, or do anything to him; for now I know that you fear God, since you have not withheld your son, your only son, from Me."** Then Abraham lifted his eyes and looked, and there behind him was a ram (Not a Lamb) caught in a thicket by its horns. So Abraham went and took the ram, and offered it up for a burnt offering instead of his son. And Abraham called the name of the place, The-LORD-Will-Provide; as it is said to this day, "In the Mount of the LORD it shall be provided."

Important firsts in the Bible happen in this scripture which need to be noted:

This is the first use of the word "love" in the Bible Genesis 22:2. GOD is describing a Father Son relationship between Abraham and Isaac as a loving relationship and later when speaking audibly about HIS son Jesus, GOD says "My beloved son, whom I love."

This is the first use of the word "Worship" in the Bible Genesis 22:4 and is Abraham's word for sacrificing his own son.

This is the first use of the repeated name "Abraham Abraham" and it only happens 7 times in the Bible and it is said by GOD.

This is the first time "GOD swears by himself" in the Bible, Genesis 22:15. The swearing is a guarantee from GOD to Abraham in recompense for Abraham not withholding his son from GOD.

GOD instructed Adam and Eve to eat of all the trees of the Garden but **not to eat** of the Tree of the Knowledge of Good and Evil and Adam and Eve went against GOD's instructions. **GOD asked** Abraham to sacrifice his son and Abraham did as he was asked. This sets up the Golden Rule, do unto others as you would have them do unto you.

Look at this exchange between Samuel and King Saul about obedience versus sacrifice:

> 1Sa 15:22 so Samuel said: "Has the LORD as great delight in burnt offerings and sacrifices, <u>**As in obeying the voice of the LORD? Behold, to obey is better than sacrifice, And to heed than the fat of rams.**</u> For rebellion is as the sin of witchcraft, And stubbornness is as iniquity and idolatry. <u>**Because you have rejected the word of the LORD, He also has rejected you**</u> from being

king." Then Saul said to Samuel, "I have sinned, **for I have transgressed the commandment of the LORD and your words, because I feared the people and obeyed their voice.**

Promise to Abraham of GOD's Promise of the Seed to come for all the nations of the earth.

Gen 22:15 Then the Angel of the LORD called to Abraham a second time out of heaven, and said: **"By Myself I have sworn, says the LORD, because you have done this thing, and have not withheld your son, your only son** blessing I will **bless you**, and multiplying I will multiply your descendants as the stars of the heaven and as the sand which is on the seashore; and your descendants shall possess the gate of their enemies. **In your seed all the nations of the earth shall be blessed, because you have obeyed My voice."**

Prophetic Attributes and Requirements on the Life and Ministry of Jesus Christ from the New Testament

Prophesy from the Angel Gabriel to Zechariah, the Priest, about His son to be "John, the Baptist".

Luke 1:11 Then an angel of the Lord appeared to him, standing on the right side of the altar of incense. And when Zacharias saw him, he was troubled, and fear fell upon him. But the angel said to him, "Do not be afraid, Zacharias, for your prayer is heard; and your wife Elizabeth will bear you a son, and you shall call his name John. And you will have joy and gladness, and many will rejoice at his birth. For he will be great in the sight of the Lord, and shall drink neither wine nor strong drink. **He will also be filled with the Holy Spirit, even from his mother's womb. And he will turn many of the children of Israel to the Lord their God. He will also go before Him in the spirit and power of Elijah, 'TO TURN THE HEARTS OF THE FATHERS TO THE CHILDREN,' and the disobedient to the wisdom of the just,** to make ready a people prepared for the Lord."

Prophesy from Angel Gabriel to Mary, the Mother of Jesus

Luke 1:24   Now after those days his wife Elizabeth conceived; and she hid herself five months, saying, "Thus the Lord has dealt with me, in the days when He looked on me, to take away my reproach among people." **Now in the sixth month the angel Gabriel was sent by God** to a city of Galilee named Nazareth, to a virgin betrothed to a man whose name was Joseph, of the house of David. The virgin's name was Mary. And having come in, the angel said to her, "Rejoice, highly favored one, the Lord is with you; blessed are you among women!" But when she saw him, she was troubled at his saying, and considered what manner of greeting this was. **Then the angel said to her, "Do not be afraid, Mary, for you** have found favor with God. And behold, you will conceive in your womb and bring forth a Son, and shall call His name JESUS. He will be great, and will be called the Son of the Highest; and the Lord God will give Him the throne of His father David. Luke 1:33 And He will reign over the house of Jacob forever, and of His kingdom there will be no end."

Angel Gabriel's word to Mary announcing miraculous information about her barren cousin Elizabeth's pregnancy added to her faith.

Luke 1:34 Then Mary said to the angel, "How can this be, since I do not know a man?" And the angel answered and said to her, "The Holy Spirit will come upon you, and the power of the Highest will overshadow you; therefore, also, that Holy One who is to be born will be called the Son of God. Now indeed, **Elizabeth your relative has also conceived a son in her old age; and this is now the sixth month for her who was called barren. For with God nothing will be impossible."**

Prophesy from Elizabeth to Mary, the Mother of Jesus.

Luke 1:41 And it happened, when Elizabeth heard the greeting of Mary, **that the babe leaped in her womb**; and Elizabeth was filled with the Holy Spirit. Then she spoke out with a loud voice and said, **"Blessed are you among women, and blessed is the fruit of your womb! But why is this granted to me, that the mother of my Lord**

should come to me? For indeed, as soon as the voice of your greeting sounded in my ears, the babe leaped in my womb for joy. Luke 1:45 **Blessed is she who believed, for there will be a fulfillment of those things which were told her from the Lord."**

Mary's song relaying the Angel's words about her Child Jesus.

Luke 1:45 **And Mary said: "My soul magnifies the Lord,** and my spirit has rejoiced in God my Savior. For He has regarded the lowly state of His maidservant; For behold, henceforth all generations will call me blessed. For He who is mighty has done great things for me, And holy is His name. And His mercy is on those who fear Him From generation to generation. He has shown strength with His arm; He has scattered the proud in the imagination of their hearts. He has put down the mighty from their thrones, And exalted the lowly. He has filled the hungry with good things, And the rich He has sent away empty. **He has helped His servant Israel, In remembrance of His mercy, As He spoke to our fathers, To Abraham and to his seed forever."** And Mary remained with her about three months, and returned to her house.

Now Elizabeth's full time came for her to be delivered, and she brought forth a son. When her neighbors and relatives heard how the Lord had shown great mercy to her, they rejoiced with her. Luke 1:59 So it was, on the eighth day, that they came to circumcise the child; and they would have called him by the name of his father, Zacharias.

Prophesy from Zechariah, the Priest about the birth of John, The Baptist.

Luke 1:67 Now his father Zacharias was filled with the Holy Spirit, and prophesied, saying: **"Blessed is the Lord God of Israel, For He has visited and redeemed His people, And has raised up a horn of salvation for us In the house of His servant David,** As He spoke by the mouth of His holy prophets, Who have been since the world began, That we should be saved from our enemies And from the hand of all who hate us, **To perform the mercy promised to our fathers And to remember His holy covenant, The oath which He swore to our father Abraham:** To grant us that we, Being delivered from the hand of our enemies, Might serve Him without fear, In holiness and righteousness before Him all the days of our life. "And you, child, will be called **the prophet of the Highest;** For you will go before the face of the Lord to prepare His ways, To give knowledge of salvation to His people By the remission of their sins, Through the tender mercy of our God, With which the Dayspring from on high has visited us; **To give light to those who sit in darkness and the shadow of death, To guide our feet into the way of peace."** Luke 1:80 So the child grew and became strong in spirit, and was in the deserts till the day of his manifestation to Israel.

Prophesy by Simeon of Jesus bringing Salvation to the Gentiles and Israel. This prophecy came at the circumcision and naming of Jesus or after Marys' purification.

Luke 2:25   And behold, there was a man in Jerusalem whose name was **Simeon, and this man was just and devout, waiting for the Consolation of Israel, and the Holy Spirit was upon him.** And it had been revealed to him by the Holy Spirit that he would not see death before he had seen the Lord's Christ. So he came by the Spirit into the temple. And when the parents brought in the Child Jesus, to do for Him according to the custom of the law, he took Him up in his arms and blessed God and said: "Lord, now You are letting Your servant depart in peace, According to Your word; **For my eyes have seen Your salvation   Which You have prepared before the face of all peoples, <u>A light to bring revelation to the Gentiles,</u> And the glory of Your people Israel."** And Joseph and His mother marveled at those things which were spoken of Him. Then Simeon blessed them, and said to Mary His mother, "Behold, this Child is destined for the fall and rising of many in Israel, and for a sign which will be spoken against (yes, a sword will pierce through your own soul also), that the thoughts of many hearts may be revealed."

Anna also prophesies about the coming of Redemption through Jesus Christ. This prophecy came after the dedication or after Mary's purification period of forty days.

> Luke 2:36 Now there was one, **Anna, a prophetess,** the daughter of Phanuel, of the tribe of Asher. She was of a great age, and had lived with a husband seven years from her virginity; and this woman was a widow of about eighty-four years, who did not depart from the temple, but served God with fastings and prayers night and day. And coming in that instant **she gave thanks to the Lord, and spoke of Him (Jesus) to all those who looked for redemption in Jerusalem.** So when they had performed all things according to the law of the Lord, they returned to Galilee, to their own city, Nazareth. And the Child grew and became strong in spirit, filled with wisdom; and the grace of God was upon Him.

The Old Testament gives us hundreds of prophesies about the coming of the Messiah. The Promise to Abraham from GOD Almighty and the giving of Jesus Christ as the Passover Lamb to take away the sin of the world, is the most important promise that we as Bible students can follow through the Bible. Jesus is the irrefutable answer to the promise.

Mathematicians have concluded that to fulfill all the

prophecies of the Bible about the first coming would take coincidences numbering 1 chance in 20,000,000,000.

What are the chances?

That there was a ram stuck in the thicket on the mountain that GOD told Abraham to sacrifice Isaac.

That Jesus would be born in Bethlehem when his parents lived in Nazareth and was prophesied 100s of years before in Micah 5:2.

That Jesus would be born to parents from the line of David.

That wise men would follow a star, probably in excess of a year, and know they were seeking to worship the New King of the Jews.

That the Messiah would be "crucified" spoken of by David in Psalm 22 when crucifixion was not a form of punishment, used by Jews. Crucifixion was invented years later by the Romans.

Chapter Two

Calendar timing parameters of
the Ministry of Jesus Christ

In Addition to the Prophetic demands, the following scriptural timing points in Jesus life set up dating requirements for the specific events in the Ministry of the Messiah, Jesus Christ. Each timing point must line up or be explained. The fulfillment of all the parameters is amazing and will build your faith in GOD's word and His Promises.

The scripture records dates that give parameters to the start and end of the first earthly Ministry of Jesus Christ.
If we allow there to be traditions that will not line up with the Bible, without explanation then our witness of GOD will be without Truth. We need to have an explanation why we celebrate Crucifixion on Good Friday and have Jesus resurrected before sunrise on Sunday morning when the Lord said he would be in the tomb three nights and three days and raised on the third day.

(1.)   The Messiah, had to start his ministry after Pontius Pilate was Governor of Judea according to Luke 3:1. And the start date cannot be earlier than **26 A.D. when Pilate received his office in the year 26 A.D**.

(2.)   The Ministry of Messiah began in 26 A.D. to agree with John 2:20, about two months after his Baptism and at the Passover Feast.

The Priests and Pharisees said, "What miraculous sign can you show us to prove your authority to do all this?" Jesus answered them, "Destroy this Temple and I will raise it again in three days" The Jews replied, "you are going to rebuild the Temple in three days and it has taken 46 years to build this Temple." But the Temple he had spoken of was his body. The Temple the Priests were speaking about started rebuilding in 19/20 BC **making this Date approximately 14 days after the start of 27 AD. This also dates the Baptism of Jesus Christ as 55 days prior to Passover.**

(3.) The Lord's Ministry, as our High Priest, could not start until Jesus was thirty years old. "Now Jesus himself was about thirty years old when he began his ministry." **The Greek word "about" here is "hosei", meaning near but not yet attained. Not "peri", the Greek word for about, vicinity, a much broader term.** Luke 3:23 When all the people were being baptized. Jesus was baptized too….v23 (Num 4:47 Priesthood could not start until age 30) **Baptism year 26 A.D.**

(4.)   By Deduction the Birth of Jesus Christ must happen in 3/2 B.C. to agree with John 2:20 and Luke 3:23.

(5.)   Jesus is 6 months younger than John, the Baptist, and therefore can be linked to date markers in the life of John. **The ministry of John, The Baptist, started in the 15th year of Tiberius Caesar (Luke 3).** According to Suetonius "Life of the twelve Caesars" Tiberius took over in 11 A.D. because of Augustus illness and by decree of the Senate became a Co-Princeps in 12 A.D. but Augustus did not die until 14 A.D. **therefore the Ministry of Jesus Christ cannot start before Late 26 A.D.**

(6.) <u>**The Passover Lamb must be a male lamb of the**</u> <u>**first year**</u> and therefore Jesus crucifixion must happen in 28 A.D. before Jesus is 32 years of age to fulfill the shadow picture of being Our Passover Lamb and High Priest. He must be over 30 years of age to be eligible to be the High Priest but not 32 years of age, to be eligible to be our lamb of the first year without spot or blemish.

<u>**(7.) The Anointed One (Jesus) must come into His**</u> <u>**ministry on Rosh Hashanah, the First Day of the first**</u> <u>**month of the year 27 AD.**</u> 483 years (Seven 7's and 62 Sevens) after the Decree went out to Ezra (Ezra 7) to Rebuild Jerusalem to fulfill Daniel 9 Prophecy. 457 BC minus 483 years plus one for the year zero = the first day of the first month of the year 27 AD to fulfill Daniel 9. This is the day Jesus walked out of the desert testing from Satan, after forty days, and John the Baptist remarked to the Pharisees as he pointed to Jesus "Behold **the Lamb of GOD** who takes away the sin of the World".

The birth date of Jesus Christ,
also, has scriptural references
that must be adhered to or explained.

(8.) **The Roman census or event commemorating** <u>**Caesar Augustus**</u> 25th year and given a new title "Father

Patrea" agrees with the Birth date of Jesus Christ. (3/2 B.C.). Luke 2 There is no record of a 3/2 BC census but many references to affirming the new title of Caesar as the Father of the Roman Empire (there were census in 8/7 BC and in 3/4 AD both these dates have fatal errors). The Roman Senate affirmation that Caesar Augustus as the Father of the Roman Empire would agree with the trip to Bethlehem for the birth of Jesus, This scenario allows The Messiah, Jesus Christ to be about 30 years old in 26 AD.

(9.) **Herod's Death** is in dispute with the more reliable point of Jesus Christ starting his ministry at Age thirty (Josephus records Herod's death as after an Eclipse before Passover which has been assumed to be March 14, 4 B.C.), but an eclipse mentioned when Herod murdered two Rabbi's is recorded as happening in 1B.C., and Herod's death was celebrated in Israel around January 10, 1B.C. And the timing of the building of the Temple lines up with Jesus being born in 3B.C. and Herod dying in 1 BC. This date in 1 B.C. is corroborated from the actions of General Varus and Sabinus linked to Herod in 1 BC, also. (Josephus Antiquities 17.9 and 17.6.2)

(10.) Luke 2:1 Jesus was born when Quirinius was Governor of Syria. Quirinius (Cyrenius) was Governor 8/7 BC and 3/4 AD, but was over the registration of the approval of Roman Senate Decree and the 750th anniversary of the founding of the Roman Empire. Oath of allegiance ordered to celebrate Augustus Caesar's silver jubilee on February 5, 2 BC. This would fit with Luke and with birth of Jesus Christ. This celebration marked the 25th anniversary of Augustus' elevation to supreme power by the Senate and people of Rome. It was also **the 750th anniversary of the founding of Rome. At this celebration, the Senate conferred upon him the title "Pater Patriae" (Father of his Country).**

The year before (3BC), Augustus sent out a decree requiring "the entire Roman people" throughout the empire to register (Census). their approval for the bestowal of this honor. This registration was required of all Roman citizens and others of distinguished rank among Rome's client kingdoms such as Judea. **Cyrenius is Governor of Syria.** Cyrenius came himself into Judea, which was now added to the province of Syria, to take an account of their substance. **Josephus - Antiquities of the Jews - Book 18.**

The complexity of compliance to each and every edict written in the Bible will become more amazing with each new category of compliance that Our GOD outlines in his Sacred Calendar, Feasts, Prophecies, Covenants, Miracles, and shadow pictures of things to come.

Jesus Christ Crucifixion at Passover
Must be on the fourth day of the week for
The tomb to be empty on the first day of the week.

The Year of the Lord's Passion **must be a year** with "the first day of the year" being the "fourth day of the week", So that the Fourteenth day of the first month can be Passover and the fourth day of the week. This is the only timing that allows the Prophecy "Three days and three nights and raised on the third day" to be fulfilled and the Tomb to be empty on the morning of the First day of the Week.

a. Only the year 28 AD has Passover on a Wednesday (fourth day of the week)
b. Year 29 Passover is on Thursday
c. Year 30 Passover is on Monday
d. Year 31 Passover is on Sunday
e. Year 32 Passover is on Thursday
f. Year 33 Passover is on Friday (The only year that fits with the Christian celebration of Good Friday)

One of the Biblical facts dating the Passion Week that provides a date certain is: When the women reached the tomb **at dawn on the first day of the week** and the tomb was empty. This starting point can allow us to build a time line based on the Spring Feasts of GOD which Jesus was celebrating and fulfilling.

Christian Passion week
Does not line up with scripture and
The requirements of the Feasts of GOD.

The Christian Passion week is based on Passover and Crucifixion occurring on Friday which has **many fatal errors** in direct conflict with other Biblical timing facts.

Passover in 33 A.D. occurs on a Friday, And mirrors the Christian Passion Week, But there are fatal errors to 33 A.D. Being the year of The Passion of Jesus

Christ.

Easter Passion week: **Control dates**
The only year with Passover on Good Friday is 33 A.D.
Fatal Errors to this year being the year of the Passion of Jesus Christ:
1. Jesus age would be from 36-40 years of age.
2. Jesus ministry would be from 6-10 years in duration
3. Jesus would not have started his ministry in the 15th year of Tiberias Caesar by 3 years.
4. The Temple would be 53 years in building instead of 46 years in verse John 2:20

Palm Sunday and the Triumphal Entry in the year 33 AD
Fatal Errors to Palm Sunday being the day of the Triumphal Entry :
1. The Triumphal Entry is part of the choosing and honoring of the Passover lamb, as the lamb is taken to the Temple to await Passover three days later. **GOD chose the tenth day of the month for the choosing of the Passover Lambs** and therefore the Triumphal Entry must always be on the tenth day of the month.
2. **The day of the choosing of the lamb is the first day of four days of Preparation for Passover and Passover is not five days from Palm Sunday as we celebrate in the Christian Passion week** (5 days). Ex 12:2

Good Friday, the "Christian Passion Week" day for the Crucifixion of Jesus Christ At the dusk on Good Friday All works stops and the Jewish weekly Sabbath starts.

Fatal Errors to Good Friday being the day of Crucifixion and Passover:

3. There **are not 3 days and 3 nights** between Friday afternoon and sunrise Sunday. And therefore the Lord's words in Luke 24:46 would be in error.

4. There is **not a day of work and commerce** for the ladies to buy spices and linen for the Lord's burial because at twilight the Weekly Sabbath starts and there is no work or commerce and the next day before dawn the women are at the Tomb to prepare the body for proper burial.

5. There is **no High Sabbath** starting GOD's Feast of Unleavened Bread spoken of in John 19:31and required in Exodus 12.

6. Jesus arrived in Bethany 6 days before Passover which would mean Jesus was walking from one city to another on the Sabbath, **which he would not do.**

Resurrection at sunrise on Sunday (The First Day of the week)

Fatal Errors to Resurrection occurring on the First day of the week:

7. There would not be enough time for the Prophesy of 3 days and 3 nights to happen and therefore the Bible would be in error.

8. If the tomb was **empty at dawn**, when the ladies reached the tomb, then Jesus had to be raised on the day before, because the scripture says 3 days and 3 nights and raised **on the third day,** not during the night.

These **"Fatal Errors"** high light the complexity of fulfilling all the requirements of the Torah, the

Prophets, and the Psalms concerning our Savior and "His First Coming". Our present celebration is based on bad facts, when a more in depth reading will reveal the beauty of GOD's promise:

- to finish transgression,
- to put an end to sin,
- to atone for wickedness,
- to bring in everlasting righteousness,
- to anoint a most Holy place.

Fulfilling all scripture, and giving us Unbreakable Promises from GOD for the "Foundation of our Faith".

**To fulfill all the demands of scripture,
Prophecies, history, and shadow pictures,
Events must happen as foretold.**

All of the following dates agree with Luke 3:1, 3:23 and John 2:20.

1. Jesus Baptism or anointing to be our High Priest must happen in the year 26 AD, Johns baptism to repentance was not necessary for Jesus to be redeemed but is part of the process of becoming a High Priest.

2. Jesus must be 30 years old in 27 AD to meet the age requirement to be a High Priest.

3. The Lord walks out of the Desert fast and testing after forty days and starts His Ministry on the first day of the first month in the year 27 AD (See note below) and

4. Jesus is Sacrificed at Passover of the year 28 AD, sixty two weeks after being Baptized, Jesus is cut off and has nothing. To fulfill Daniel 9.

5. Our Lord is raised from the Dead at the end of the Sabbath (17th day) in the year 28 AD, and delivers the First Fruits offering to His Father on the First Day of the week Nissan 18, 28 AD.

6. Forty days later, The Lord ascends to be with his Father

7. Ten Days after the ascension, The Father God sends the Holy Spirit to bring power and leadership to the Church at Pentecost 490 days after The Lord's Baptism or Anointing.

The only year that will meet all the demands of the scripture, for the year, that Jesus was sacrificed for our sins is the Year 28 AD.

Dates from scripture and history get us close to identifying the date of the Crucifixion, and the Shadow pictures and Feast requirements confirm the date of Jesus crucifixion on Passover and Passover being the fourth day of the week and only the year 28AD has Passover on the fourteenth day of the month. (within a reasonable number of years)

Note:
The Daniel 9:24 prophecy announcing that the Anointed One will come 483 years after the "Decree to Rebuild Jerusalem" The only decree with a date from which to track time is the Ezra 7 decree. The Decree from Artexerxes is in the year 457 which calculates 483 years to the first day of the first month in the year 27 AD. The day Jesus walked out of the desert after a forty day testing on the first day of the first month of 27 AD and John, the Baptist, exclaimed to Pharisees questioning him, "Behold the Lamb of GOD that takes away the sin of the world".

Ezra 7:8 And Ezra came to Jerusalem in the fifth month, which was in **the seventh year of the king. On the first day of the first month** he began his journey from Babylon, and on the first day of the fifth month he came to Jerusalem, according to the good hand of his God upon him. For Ezra had prepared his heart to seek the Law of the LORD, and to do it, and to teach statutes and ordinances in Israel. Ezra This is a copy of the letter that King Artaxerxes gave Ezra the priest, the scribe, expert in the words of the commandments of the LORD, and of His statutes to Israel: Ezra Artaxerxes, king of kings, To Ezra the priest, a scribe of the Law of the God of heaven: Perfect peace, and so forth. Ezra 7:13 **I issue a decree** that all those of the people of Israel and the priests and Levites in my realm, who volunteer to go up to Jerusalem, may go with you.

In one hundred and seven years, there are four edicts from Kings to Ezra and Nehemiah allowing them to return to Jerusalem with volunteers to rebuild their city. Only the edicts given to Ezra are a "decree" which is the same word as used by Gabriel when Gabriel gave the prophesy to Daniel and it is Ezra 6:3 and 7:13. But only the decree in 7:13 has a traceable starting date, which corresponds to the first day of the year in 27 AD. The date is important because the Prophesy given to Daniel must have a starting date. The decree in Ezra 7:13 is 58 years after the completion of the Temple but before the Walls and Gates of Jerusalem were started and all work had come to a stop for these 58 years. Therefore, Jesus Walked out of the Desert experience on the first day of the first month of the year 27 AD.

Exact dates for the Feasts of GOD
Spoken by GOD to Moses

These Feasts, are not feasts set up by the High Priest or the Jewish Government. These Feasts were commanded by GOD to be celebrated "forever", The Feasts are GOD's time to meet with His People. Those who are unclean for any reason may celebrate one month later, but there does not appear to be any excuse accepted for not celebrating GOD's Feasts.

These are GOD's words to Moses
regarding His Feasts:

Exo 12:3 Speak to all the congregation of Israel, saying: **'On the tenth of this month** every man shall take for himself a lamb, according to the house of his father, a lamb for a household.

Exo 12:6 **Now you shall keep it until the fourteenth day of the same month. Then the whole assembly of the congregation of Israel shall kill it at twilight.**

Exo 12:15 Seven days you shall eat unleavened bread. On the first day you shall remove leaven from your houses. For whoever eats leavened bread from the first day until the seventh day, that person shall be cut off from Israel.

Exo 12:16 **On the first day there shall be a holy convocation,** and on the seventh day there shall be a holy convocation for you. No manner of work shall be done on them; but that which everyone must eat—that only may be prepared by you. Exo 12:17 So you shall observe the Feast of Unleavened Bread, for on this same day I will have brought your armies out of the land of Egypt. Therefore you shall observe this day throughout your generations as an everlasting ordinance.

Lev 23:6 **And on the fifteenth day of the same month the Feast of Unleavened Bread to the LORD begins;** seven days you must eat unleavened bread.
Lev 23:9 And the LORD spoke to Moses, saying, Lev 23:10 "Speak to the children of Israel, and say to them: 'When you come into the land which I give to you, **and reap its harvest, then you shall bring a sheaf of the first fruits of your harvest to the priest.** Lev 23:11 He shall wave the sheaf before the LORD, to be accepted on your behalf; on **the day after the Sabbath** the priest shall wave it. Lev 23:12 And you shall offer on that day, when you wave the sheaf, **a male lamb of the first year, without blemish, as a burnt offering to the LORD.** Lev 23:13 Its grain offering shall be two-tenths of an ephah of fine flour mixed with oil, an offering made by fire to the LORD, for a sweet aroma; and its drink offering shall be of wine, one-fourth of a hin. Lev

23:14 You shall eat neither bread nor parched grain nor fresh grain until the same day that you have brought an offering to your God; it shall be **a statute forever** throughout your generations in all your dwellings. Lev 23:15 And you shall count for yourselves **from the day after the Sabbath,** from the day that you brought the sheaf of the wave offering: seven Sabbaths shall be completed. The next day is 50 days or as it is called Pentecost (Shavuots in Hebrew).

The scriptural framework of for the timing of GOD's Feasts are exact and we must examine each part of the Passion to see the beauty of GOD's demands and Jesus fulfillment of each and every requirement.

- Choosing of our Passover Lamb must be on the 10th day
- Triumphal entry must be on the 10th day
- Three days of Feast preparation
- Killing the lamb must be at twilight on the 14th day
- Feast of Unleavened Bread starts on the 15th
- First Fruits offering must be on the 1st day of the week

Chapter Three

The Foundational scriptures
Delineating the timing of the "Passion weeks".

Jesus Christ said, **"I have not come to abolish the Law (Torah) and the Prophets but to fulfill them." Let us examine the fulfillment by Jesus Christ**, of the Feast of Passover, Unleavened Bread, and First Fruits Offering.

The Christian "Passion week" is not founded on "The Sacred Feasts of GOD" and therefore is missing the incredible beauty of GOD's fulfillment of HIS Spring Feasts. Our Christian forefathers have created Easter traditions around the seven to 15 stations of the Cross (if you include the stations inside the Church of the Sepulcher), the Via Dolorosa, and Lent and others.

The word "Easter" only appears in the Bible once and it is a poor translation. The word Pesach, Pesah, (Paschal Greek) is the word for Passover in the entire New Testament except the one time in Acts when it is translated "Easter". Easter was not celebrated until mid-second century after one hundred plus years after Jesus death, **therefore Jesus was not fulfilling any aspect of "Easter".**

The question with the timing of the Christian "Passion week of Jesus Christ" is that **Jesus Christ, a Jew**, is participating in GOD's <u>Feast of Passover, Unleavened Bread, and the First Fruits offering</u>, **not Easter.** Exodus 12 gives the exact timing for each day of the Feasts. The specific Feast days integral to the Spring Feasts, that we do not acknowledge, in our worship, called Easter, is the High Sabbath of Unleavened Bread and The First Fruits offering on the First day of the week. **The High Sabbath beginning the Feast of Unleavened Bread begins at the end of the Passover Meal and must be the 15th day of the month and is a day in which "there is no work" except to prepare meals.**

**The following questions and answers
help to illustrate the exact timing of
the Passion Week according to
GOD's Sacred Calendar.**

1. Do you believe the women found the tomb empty **at first light on the First day of the week?**
　　　　If you believe the women arrived at the tomb, as scripture says (Matt 28:1), **at first light,** we have a solid time juncture (a date and time) to build a time line for the Passion Week. This empty tomb fact, tells us that Jesus was resurrected before first light on the first day of the week. **It does not tell us that he was resurrected on the first day of the week.**

2. Do you believe that Jesus was in the tomb **three nights and three days and raised on the third day?**
　　　　If you believe **the most repeated prophecy** in the Bible, that Jesus was in the tomb for three nights and three days and raised on the third day, **spoken by the Lord, Himself, then logic would dictate that Jesus was**

resurrected on the Sabbath at the end of the daytime and the discovery of His resurrection happened the next morning at first light on the First day of the week because the Tomb was empty. Additionally, we can deduce the Weekly Sabbath must be the 17th day of the month.

3. Do you believe **Jesus is our Passover lamb** and was sacrificed for our sins?

If you believe that Jesus is our Passover lamb and was sacrificed for our sins, as scripture says (1Cor. 5:7), then we have **reason to believe that Jesus was sacrificed on Passover,** confirmed by the information that within hours after the Crucifixion, the evening starting with the Passover meal, which begins the High Sabbath of Unleavened Bread. John 19:31

4. Do you believe that **Passover takes place on the Fourteenth day of the month?**

If you believe that the Passover takes place on the fourteenth day of the Month, as scripture decrees (Ex. 12:6), then we have reason to believe that after Passover there must be three nights and three days before The First day of the week, when it was discovered that Jesus had been resurrected. Therefore counting as the Hebrews would have done, at that time, with each day starting at twilight, Three nights and three days would make the date of Resurrection the 17th day of the month. And "raised on the third day" narrows the time line down to the daytime before the evening starting the First day of the week, CONFIRMED BY the women arriving at the tomb before light on the First day of the week and the Tomb was empty.

5. Do you believe that the **High Sabbath of Unleavened Bread** is celebrated on the fifteenth day of the month?

If you believe that GOD's decree (Lev. 23:6) that the first day of the Feast of Unleavened Bread is to be a **High Sabbath and follows Passover** and is on the Fifteenth day of the month, then the crucifixion, death, and burial of our Lord must be prior to the start of the High Sabbath, because there can be no work, trial, execution, or burial after the High Sabbath begins.

6. Do you believe **Jesus Christ is our High Priest and has duties to perform as our High Priest?**

Hebrews 5:5-7 Scriptures indicate that there is a new High Priest for the New Covenant and greater sacrifices than bulls and goats are necessary to be presented at the Heavenly Temple. Therefore the First Fruits offering for the New Covenant must be made by the new High Priest in the Heavenly Temple on the First day of the week. Additional scriptures Daniel 9 Anoint a most Holy Place and Exodus 40:10.

7. Do you believe that **Jesus Christ, our High Priest, delivered the First Fruits offering** to His Father in Heaven, on the First Day of the Week?

If you believe that we have such a High Priest, Scripture tells us after He had risen from the dead, **He who was "the firstborn from the dead"** (Colossians 1:18), **delivered to His Father the "first fruits of them that slept"** (1 Corinthians 15:20), that His disciples, and indeed all who would "believe on |Him| through their word" (John 17:20), could be made "sons of God" (Romans 8:14). "And if children, then heirs; heirs of God, and joint heirs with Christ" (Romans 8:17). This high standing comes as a fulfillment of His determination to "be the firstborn among many brethren" (v. 29). And we, who believe, are the many brethren (The Church).

8. **Why was the Veil to the Holy of Holies "ripped" from top to bottom** at the exact time Jesus Christ became our Sacrifice for sin, bringing in Everlasting Righteousness?

       In the Hebrew community, the High Priest went in to the Holy of Holies once a year on the Day of Atonement to sprinkle blood on the Ark of the Covenant for the sins of the Nation of Israel for the year.

> Heb 9:11 **But Christ came as High Priest of the good things to come,** with the greater and more perfect tabernacle not made with hands, that is, not of this creation. HE did not enter with the blood of goats and calves, **but with His own blood He entered the Most Holy Place once for all, having obtained eternal redemption.**

Fulfillment of GOD's word and the shadow picture GOD painted happened in a split second. The death of our Savior **instantly gave believers** entrance into to GOD's presence "The Holiest of Holies" and as an Earthly sign Father GOD ripped the Veil separating HIM from HIS People from the top to the bottom.

9. **Why could Mary not touch Jesus in the Garden** on the First day of the week and later that night Jesus allowed

the disciples in the Upper room to touch Him.

If you said Jesus was male chauvinists, you would be wrong. The key is that Jesus Christ, acting as our High Priest, **had not ascended to His Father with his First Fruits offering.** Ask yourself what happened to the Holy ones who arose when he arose? John 20:14…Jesus said "Mary!" …... **Do not touch me, because I have NOT YET ASCENDED TO MY FATHER.** Later that same day Jesus returned, after ascending to the Father, appeared to the disciples on the road to Emmaus and then to the upper room where the disciples were gathered and Jesus let the disciples touch Him. John 20:26…. Jesus came and stood among them and said "Peace be with you" then he said to Thomas, "Put your fingers here and see my hands; reach out your hand and put it in my side". (One gospel indicates the experience with Thomas is a week later.)

10. What happened to the "Holy Ones" who were resurrected as Jesus was resurrected and came out of their graves and were seen in the city by people who recognized them? Matthew 27:51-54

If you believe that they went back in there graves you would be wrong because "Resurrected Saints" will not die twice. They went to Heaven with Jesus, our High Priest, as part of the First Fruits offering of those who slept, being part of the fulfillment of the First Fruits Wave Offering by Jesus Christ, our new High Priest, on the first day of the week.

These questions and answers point out the necessary timing of the Passion Week according to the Bible and GOD's

Sacred Calendar.

Scriptural Framework
that must be maintained

This section sets out scriptural framework for the Passion weeks that must be maintained for the Bible to be inerrant and to confirm the interaction of all the facts and requirements set out in the Bible with the culture of the time.

The Bible confirms that "The tomb" was empty prior to the women reaching the tomb at first light, on the first day of the week Matt. 28:1-8, Mark 16:1-8, Luke 24:1-12, and John 20:1-8 Roman and Hebraic history also, records the empty tomb.

Four important facts established by the timing of the discovery of the empty tomb;
1. Timing of the resurrection **was prior to dawn at the First day of the week.**
2. Timing of the entombment period, "three nights and three days and **raised on the third day**", this fact tells us the Resurrection must be in the daytime.
3. Crucifixion must happen prior to Thursday or the fifth day of the week.
4. Resurrection must be at the end of the Sabbath Day.
        * According to all four Gospels the women arrived at the tomb at the dawn and he (Jesus) was not in the tomb but later in the longer version of Mark 16:9 It is announced "Jesus having risen early in the morning of the first day of

the week he appeared first to Mary. This being in contradiction to verse Mark 16:1-7. **If you read or punctuate the verse** "Jesus having risen, (comma or period) Early in the morning of the first day of the week appeared first to Mary". This reading of the verse does not contradict itself with verse Mark 16:1-7 and the other Gospels.

The most repeated prophecy in the Bible is "three nights and three days and raised on the third day. Matt16:21, Luke 18:33, Luke 24:46, Acts 10:40 and many more.

Four important facts affecting the entombment time period.

1. There can be **no trials, executions, or burials** after twilight starting **GOD's Feast of Unleavened Bread** on the fifteenth day of the month, which is a High Sabbath. The High Sabbath starts as soon as there are three stars visible usually during the Passover meal and starts an evening and day **without work.**
2. Three nights and days (72 hours) and raised on the third day starts with the burial at the end of the Passover day and the resurrection happening at the evening ending the Weekly Sabbath.
3. <u>**Passover lambs are sacrificed at twilight on Passover and before the High Sabbath of Unleavened Bread starts.**</u>
4. Work and commerce are allowable on **the evening and day** after the High Sabbath and before the evening starting

the Weekly Sabbath. For Example, the women could buy linen and perfumed oils, with which, to wrap Jesus body and the Priests could meet with the Gentile Romans to ask for a Guard for the Tomb as soon as the High Sabbath was over. Mark 16:1 Now when the Sabbath was past (High Sabbath), Mary Magdalene, Mary the mother of James, and Salome **bought spices,** that they might come and anoint Him. This has to be on the preparation day to the Weekly Sabbath because they are at the Tomb on the first day of the week before dawn to anoint the body with oil, they bought, after the High Sabbath of Unleavened Bread and before the Weekly Sabbath.

The Bible confirms that Jesus is our Passover Lamb.
1Cor 5:7 For indeed Christ, our Passover, was sacrificed for us.
Four important facts about Passover that determine Passion Week timing.
1. Passover by GOD's decree is celebrated on the fourteenth day of the month.
2. Jesus is our Passover Lamb and is sacrificed on Passover.
3. Passover is a day of work because the Passover Lamb is sacrificed.
4. John 19:31 Therefore, because it was the (High Sabbath) Preparation Day, that the bodies **should not remain** on the cross on the Sabbath (**for that Sabbath was a high day**), the Jews asked Pilate that their legs might be broken, and that they might be taken away. (To speed up the death for those on the crucifix's.) This scripture confirms that Jesus Christ died on the day before the High Sabbath of

Unleavened bread and was in the tomb before the Passover meal.

The Bible gives readers an incredible picture of the First Fruits offering and its timing, and the Lord's presentation of the First Fruits to His Father in Heaven.

Follow carefully the wording and timing:
The scripture reports as Jesus gave up His Spirit
"Then, behold, the veil of the temple was torn in two from top to bottom; and
the earth quaked, and
the rocks were split, **and**
the graves were opened; and
many bodies of the saints who had fallen asleep
were raised; and (THREE DAYS Later)
coming out of the graves after His resurrection,
they went into the holy city and appeared to many."
Matt 27:51-54

Seven Important facts about the First Fruits offering and Jesus Christ our High Priest.
1. The Spring feasts around Passover are at the Harvest of Barley and the Priest pick out the finest sampling (10 shocks) of the crop to be used for the First Fruits Wave offering.
2. The First Fruits of the Harvest are marked for the offering as soon as the Last Passover lamb is sacrificed. The Priest tie ten shocks together, **they do Not harvest** "just mark" as the First Fruits of the Harvest. It is marked

on the day the Passover lambs are sacrificed because it is a day of work and because the barley chosen has to be ripe and without blemish, so it can be harvested at the end of the day of the Weekly Sabbath for the Offering to the Lord on the First day of the Week. At this same time the Graves of the Holy Ones **were opened and marked.**

3. The First Fruits of the Barley will be harvested right after the Weekly Sabbath ends. The Priests work through the night to harvest, separate from its husk, and process the Barley for the "Wave Offering" along with a Lamb of the first year without spot or blemish for the "Sin Offering".
And they (the Holy Ones) were resurrected as Jesus was resurrected and were seen in town by others.

4. Caiaphas, High Priest will offer the First Fruits offering to the Lord on the First Day of the Week in the Earthly Temple.

5. **Jesus Christ, our High Priest, will ascend to the Father with the first Fruits offering of Himself (a lamb of the first year without spot or blemish) and the First Fruits of them that slept. (The Saints who were resurrected)**

6. **Consider, The Saints** that were resurrected and were seen in Town. The Graves were opened (marked) at Jesus Christ death and "the Saints" were raised at HIS Resurrection (just like the First Fruits of the Barley). The bones had to have muscle, sinew, organs, skin, blood, water, **and everything needed to be resurrected and to be recognized in town. Matt 27:51-54**

7. Hebrews tells us that the Resurrected Saints and Jesus Christ were at the Heavenly Temple during the First Fruits offering time on the First day of the week. "Now this is

how the copies of **the heavenly things had to be purified,** but the heavenly things themselves require **better sacrifices** than these. Hebrews 9:24 For the Messiah has entered a Holiest Place which is not man-made and merely a copy of the true one, **but into heaven itself, in order to appear now on our behalf in the very presence of God."** **1Corinthians 15:20, Ephesians 1:20, Colossians 1:18**

Each requirement and fact revealed in GOD's Word has further ramifications that complicate the chronology and information we are not given directly. For one Example: The Saints (Holy Ones) who were resurrected were given new bodies because they were recognized in Town. Also, because they are specifically called "Saints" and not just the dead, this helps confirm that they are First Fruits of them that slept. Only GOD can orchestrate this miracle. As GOD said to Ezekiel

> Eze 37:4 Again He said to me, "Prophesy to these bones, and say to them, 'O dry bones, hear the word of the LORD! Thus says the Lord GOD to these bones: **"Surely I will cause breath to enter into you, and you shall live.**
>
> I will put sinews on you and bring flesh upon you, cover you with skin and put breath in you; and you shall live. Then you shall know that I am the LORD." '"So I prophesied as I was commanded; and as I prophesied, there was a noise, and suddenly a rattling; and the bones came together, bone to bone. Indeed, as I looked, the sinews and the flesh came upon them, and the skin covered

them over; but there was no breath in them. Also He said to me, "Prophesy to the breath, prophesy, son of man, and say to the breath, 'Thus says the Lord GOD: "Come from the four winds, O breath, and breathe on these slain, that they may live."

"'So I prophesied as He commanded me, and breath came into them, and they lived, and stood upon their feet, an exceedingly great army. Then He said to me, "Son of man, these bones are the whole house of Israel. They indeed say, 'Our bones are dry, our hope is lost, and we ourselves are cut off!' Therefore prophesy and say to them, 'Thus says the Lord GOD: **Behold, O My people, I will open your graves and cause you to come up from your graves, and bring you into the land of Israel.** Eze 37:13 **Then you shall know that I am the LORD, when I have opened your graves, O My people, and brought you up from your graves.**

This resurrection is also talked about in Rev. 11:11.

**Three approaches
to the required timing of the
Spring Feasts of GOD**

Exact days chosen by GOD for HIS Feasts (Exodus 12)

1. The Triumphal entry must be on the **10th day of the month.**

The Passion of the Christ, 47

2. **There must be three additional days of Feast preparation**
3. The Passover & crucifixion must be on the **14th day of the month.**
4. **The High Sabbath of Unleavened Bread must be on the 15th day of the month.**
5. **There must be three days and three nights between Crucifixion and the Weekly Sabbath this year.**
6. First Fruits offering must be on the First Day of the week.
7. The total number of days in the GOD's Feast Schedule is 9 days and in the Christian "Passion week" is 8 days. This schedule happens every year that Passover is on a Wednesday. Also Passover must be on a Wednesday and the 14th day of the month, to fulfill the Prophesy of "three days and nights and raised on the third day", the most repeated prophesy in the New Testament.
8. The only year that Passover is on the Fourth day of the week and Jesus is in his thirty-first year is 28 AD.

The Scriptural timing of Passover, the Feast of Unleavened Bread, and First Fruits:

1. There can only be four days between the triumphant entry and Crucifixion, Exodus 12:2
2. There must be three days and three nights in the entombment period. Luke 24:7
3. Jesus must be raised on the third day. Luke 24:46
4. There must be a High Sabbath after Passover and before the weekly Sabbath. Exodus 12:16
5. The First Fruits must be marked for harvest at the end of Passover because it is an act of work so it must be done

right after the Passover Lamb is sacrificed and before the day ends.

6. First Fruits offering must be made on the first day of the week because the counting of the Omer must include seven Sabbaths and one day and be 50 days from the First Fruits offering to The Feast of Pentecost "Shavuots".

Detailed timing of the Month of the Aviv (Nisan) and the Feasts of GOD in 28 AD:

The New Year (Rosh Hashanah) starts with the sighting of the renewed moon in the month the barley is ripe. Exodus 12:1 details the days and events of the Spring Feasts of the LORD. There are four Sabbaths in the Jewish Passover, Unleavened Bread, and First Fruits Offering. Two are High Sabbaths marking the First day and Last Day of the Feast following Passover sacrifice and two are Weekly Sabbaths in the year 28 AD.

*10th day of the Month: "The Passover Lamb" is chosen and paraded to the Temple. (Weekly Sabbath with no work except by Divine instruction)

11th day: The lambs and households are cleaned and washed

12th day: The children are taught about GOD's deliverance of Israel from slavery.

13th day: Prepare the table, clothes, each person, and the feast to await the lamb.

14th day: Passover Lamb is sacrificed at twilight and eaten with bitter herbs and unleavened bread.

*15th day: The first day of the Feast of

Unleavened Bread (High Sabbath, an evening and day with no work)

16th day: The second day of the Feast of Unleavened Bread (Day of Preparation for the Weekly Sabbath) In a different year there could be up to five more days of preparation if the 15th day of the month was on the first day of the week.

*17th day: The third day of the Feast of Unleavened Bread (Weekly Sabbath with no work)

18th day: The day of First Fruits offering, the day after the Weekly Sabbath.

19th day: Fifth day of the Feast of Unleavened Bread

20th day: Preparation for the High Sabbath ending First Fruits

*21st day: The Last day (High Sabbath with no work)

*Denotes a Sabbath, Weekly or High Sabbath required by GOD's Feast timing.

Chapter Four

A Daily Comparison of Jesus actions at the Passion week and The High Priest and The Feasts of GOD from Passover through the First Fruits offering.

Virtually everything that happened to the Passover lamb also happened to Jesus Christ but the temporary benefit for the sacrifice of the lamb was replaced with the permanent sacrifice for sin by Jesus Christ. The Atonement provided by Jesus Christ was supernatural and HIS sacrifice for sin was made once for all, for the past, present, and future.

The excitement of the Passion Week's triumphal entry of the Passover Lamb was indescribable in the year 28 AD for several unusual reasons;
1. The Hebrew Nation was aware of **Jesus doing two miracles that, no other person claiming to be The Messiah, had ever done;** the raising of Lazarus from the dead, after four days, and the healing of a man born blind.
2. Hundreds of thousands, if not a million Hebrew pilgrims were in Jerusalem to meet with their GOD and were lined up to welcome **the High Priest as he brings the "Passover lamb"** through the streets from Bethlehem to be kept at the Temple for 4 days until Passover.
3. **The Hebrew pilgrims in Jerusalem were trying to see the "King" they had been anticipating to redeem Israel and deliver them out of Roman occupation and control.** Could this be the year of GOD's deliverance, again like deliverance from Egypt?

4. The Hebrew ruling body, teachers of the Torah, Pharisees, and Sadducees are seized with fear of losing their positions and power, and therefore plot to kill Jesus and Lazarus. **Lazarus was a Pharisee and just being alive is a testimony to Jesus being, The Messiah.**

Consider the matrix of cultures and constituencies, **the scene is set for The Messiah, Jesus Christ, to enter the city and fulfill the Father's Promises, and be the Passover lamb, and our Savior.** The following schedule compares the Christian and Jewish Passion Weeks to illustrate the differences. Jesus Christ was the fulfillment to both the worldly and Heavenly System of the Spring Feasts of the LORD.

<u>**10th   day of the month of Aviv**</u> (Nisan) 1st day of preparation for Passover and the day for choosing the Passover lamb for each family and the High Priest choosing a lamb for the Hebrew Nation.

(1) **The High Priest goes to Bethlehem to choose the Passover Lamb for the nation and a lamb for the First Fruits sin offering,** the Priests then bring the lambs back to the streets filled with pilgrims with palm fronds and cedar boughs crowded into the streets of Jerusalem yelling "Hosanna, Blessed is he who comes in the name of the Lord, Hosanna, Peace in the Heavens and Glory in the highest. Hosanna, Blessed is he who comes in the name of the Lord, Blessed is the King of Israel"

> (1a) **This year (28 AD) Jesus Christ, Lord of the Sabbath, and born in Bethlehem, enters**

Jerusalem in triumph on a donkey's colt to the praises of the people in attendance at the Feasts on the tenth day of the Month, on the Sabbath, fulfilling Zechariah 9:9 and spoken of in Matthew 21:1-9 & John 12:12-16.

(2) John 12:12 ... the great crowd that had come for the feast, heard that Jesus was on his way to Jerusalem, **they took out palm branches and went out to meet him shouting "Hosanna, Blessed is he who comes in the name of the Lord, Blessed is the King of Israel"** (Psalm 118:25-27)

> (2a) **At the same time the crowd was waiting for the High Priest to return, from Bethlehem, with the Passover lamb** to be sacrificed for Israel's sins. This year the High Priest enters after The Messiah. The High Priest was accompanied by a host of priests and Levites. Upon entrance to the city, the pilgrims there for the feasts would shake their branches and shout "Hosanna, Blessed is he who comes in the name of the Lord, Blessed is the King of Israel" This had been done for over 1000 years.

11th, 12th, and 13th days of the month – three additional days of Preparation for the Feasts of GOD
The cleansing or the homes of all leaven (Sin) and Jesus cleansing the Temple of moneychangers.

The children learn questions to ask about GOD's deliverance; Jesus spends four days talking and teaching about GOD's deliverance in the Temple and in the evening in the Garden of Gethsemane, ending with the teaching and prayer after the "Last Supper".

14th day of the month – **"Passover"   The beginning of Passover started at dusk during the Last Supper. Then the Garden teaching and prayer experience, arrest, trials, scourging, crucifixion, and burial followed.**

(3) The priest as he prepared to sacrifice the Passover Lambs inspected them for spot or blemish and said **"I find no fault** (each Lamb)" and then the sacrifice is made.

> (3A) Pilate and Herod said at the trial, of Jesus, each conducted, **"I find no fault in HIM"** Luke 23:13-14
>
> (3b) Jesus death from crucifixion ended at the same time, as the Jewish families sacrifice the Passover Lambs at twilight on Passover.

(4) The High Priest after sacrificing the last lamb informs the attendees **"it is finished"**

> (4a) Jesus after completing his task on the cross says **"It is Finished"**

The Lord's Crucifixion is the fulfillment of the picture of our Passover Lamb, a lamb of the first year without spot or blemish.

> 4(b) During the sacrifice of the of the Passover lambs **as the Lord dismissed his Spirit,** the Veil separating Holy place from the Holy of Holies and the Presence of GOD was rent from top to bottom.
>
> (4c) (While Jesus is being put in the earthen tomb)

The high Priest, after taking the Passover lamb downstairs under the Temple, to be roasted for the Passover Meal, **the High Priest resurfaces and with a large party of priests and attendees goes over by the Mount of Olives to mark or bind together 10 shocks of Barley for the First Fruits offering.** The marking of the Barley for the First Fruits offering must be done quickly, because the High Sabbath starting Unleavened Bread is about to start and all work must stop.

(5) Then the High Priest stays in seclusion for three days and three nights **until the First Fruits are harvested at the end of the Sabbath.** The Priests and a large group of Pilgrims harvest the barley and then work through the night to prepare the barley for the wave offering on the first day of the week along with a spotless lamb of the first year for the Sin offering.

> (5a) At Jesus death, the earth quaked **and the tombs on the Mount of Olives were opened and marked (Just as the High Priest marked the barley for the First Fruits offering.).** Then Jesus entombment period began, three nights and three days until his resurrection at the end of the Sabbath. Matt 27:51-54

Three days later

> (5b) and "then" **the Holy ones in the graves were resurrected (and given recognizable bodies) as he (Jesus) was resurrected and the Saints showed themselves to people in the city.** The

Holy ones are the First Fruits offering along with a spotless lamb of the first year to be delivered to the Father on the first day of the week. Matt 27:51-54

When Jesus is sacrificed, he is over 30 years of age, the age requirement to be a High Priest, and is not 32 years of age so that he is a lamb of the first year.

(After Twilight the High Sabbath of Unleavened Bread starts and their cannot be any work except meal preparation)

Entombment period for our Savior
Nisan 15,   **Night and Day (1)**
        High Sabbath of Unleavened Bread
Nisan 16, Preparation day,   **Night and Day (2)**
        (6) Women buy spices and perfumes and prepare them to anoint the Body of The Lord and rest through the Sabbath.
        (6A) Priests go to Romans to ask for a Guard for the Tomb because Jesus said he would rise on the third day.

Nisan 17, Weekly Sabbath   **Night and day (3)**
Right after the twilight, between The Weekly Sabbath and the First day of the Week, when work is allowed.
        (7) First Fruits of the barley, **marked as First Fruits before the High Sabbath of Unleavened Bread,** to be harvested, after the weekly Sabbath, by the High Priest, priests and attendees. At the end of the Weekly Sabbath, a large group of

Priests and Pilgrims assemble on the Mount of Olives to watch the harvesting and to prepare the barley for the First Fruits Wave Offering, in the morning, at first prayers. The First Fruits of the barley is offered to the Lord along with a lamb of the first year without spot or blemish.

(7a) Jesus harvests the tombs of the Holy ones on the Mount of Olives, **The graves marked when the earth quaked as Jesus died Matt 27:51 As he was resurrected (three days later),** they (Holy ones in the tombs) were resurrected and were seen by hundreds in the city (and probably the priests and attendees watching the harvesting of the barley). Another shadow picture fulfilled in the First Fruits offering, The First Fruits of them that slept.

Nisan 18,   **First day of the week**
First Fruits offering at morning Prayers

(8) Day of the First Fruits wave offering Leviticus 23:9

Priests prepare barley through the night for the First Fruits Wave offering on the morning of the First day of the week along with a spotless lamb of the first year.

(8a) **Resurrected Saints** were resurrected and seen in town. Mat 27:51

At Dawn, Mary and the other women **bring the spices to the tomb** to anoint the body of Jesus but the Tomb is empty.

(8b) **Jesus meets Mary and won't let her touch**

him (John 20:14) <u>because he has not yet ascended to his Father</u>. Not allowing Mary to touch Him does not make since unless you are familiar with First Fruits offering because Jesus allows Thomas to touch him later (John 20:26). **Jesus Christ is about to take the Resurrected saints, to his Father in the Heavenly Temple as his first fruits offering** (see 1Corinthians 15:21-22 and Hebrews 9:23) **at the same time the priests are offering the first fruits of the barley and a spotless lamb in the earthly Temple of GOD.** Jesus returns to earth in hours to meet the disciples on the road to Emmaus. Later that night Jesus allows the disciples in the upper room to touch him.

(8c) But it was not until He had risen from the dead, He who was "the firstborn from the dead" (Colossians 1:18), **delivered to His Father the "first fruits of them that slept"** (1 Corinthians 15:20), that His disciples, and indeed all who would "believe on |Him| through their word" (John 17:20), could be made "sons of God". what is the exceeding greatness of His power toward us who believe, according to the working of His mighty power Eph 1:20 which He worked in Christ when He raised Him from the dead and seated Him at His right hand in the heavenly places.

Every requirement of GOD's "old covenant" to cover Israel's sins for the past year and offer the first fruits of their harvest, Jesus Christ fulfilled. Specifically HE

fulfilled the Triumphal Entry, Death at Passover, Resurrection at end of Weekly Sabbath, and delivery of First Fruits offering on the First day of the week to bring about Everlasting Righteousness to those who believe, past, present, and future.

Chapter Five

Hour by Hour Analysis of
The Lord Jesus Christ fulfillment of Prophecy and
GOD's Feasts based on the Hebrew Calendar
With the days starting at dusk

The following section detailing the movements of Jesus Christ by the hour are not meant to be exact but are to be used to contrast the culture of the actual Passion Week and the Modern day Passion week. The comparison based on the Spring Feasts of GOD, the Feasts schedule Jesus Christ was there to celebrate, NOT Easter which was added to Christianity over 100 years later.

Six days before Passover
Fifth day of the week

On the way up from Jericho, Jesus came to the east side of the Mount of Olives where Bethany and Bethphage were located. From there the road skirted the south end of Olivet, dipped into the Valley of Jehoshaphat, crossed the Kidron Brook and climbed up to Jerusalem. John 12:1-8; **Six days before the Passover.** Jesus arrived in Bethany where Lazarus lived, whom Jesus had raised from the dead. Jesus had been traveling from Jericho to Bethany, and probably arrived in the afternoon at the end of the Jewish day.

Note: The Jewish day started at evening and was calculated "night then day".

Five Days before Passover
Sixth day of the week.

Assuming that Jesus had started from Jericho early in the morning, the walk of more than 12 miles as the crow flies would have taken most of the day. He would have arrived late in the day and at the evening meal the new day started in the Jewish culture.

6:PM Night approaches and it is <u>the beginning of the 9th day of the month and the 6th day of the week.</u>
7:PM And the meal at the family home of Mary, Martha, and Lazarus in Bethany continues.
8:PM
9:PM
10:PM
11:PM   Overnight
12:PM
1:AM
2:AM
3:AM
4:AM
5:AM
6:AM Luke 21:37 Yeshua spent his days at the Temple, teaching; while at night he went out and stayed on the hill called the Mount of Olives. Luke 21:38 All the people would rise with the dawn to come and hear him at the Temple courts. Luke 22:1 But the festival of Matzah (Unleavened Bread), known as Pesach (Passover), was approaching;
7:AM
8:AM

9:AM
10:AM
11:AM
12:AM
1:PM
2:PM
3:PM   Luke 19:29 **As they approached Bethany,** Jesus
sent two disciples saying "Go into the village ahead of you,
as you enter it you will find a colt tied there, which no one
has ever ridden, bring it here. If anyone ask you "why are
you untying it? Tell them the Lord needs it." Luke tells us
(where John did not) that the Lord rides the colt into town
in the Triumphal Entry. Preparing to fulfill the prophesy of
Zechariah 9:9. "Tell the daughter of Zion, 'Behold, your
King is coming to you, Lowly, and sitting on a donkey, a
colt, the foal of a donkey.'"
4:PM
5:PM   Here a dinner was given in Jesus honor, two
Gospels indicate this meal is two evenings later.... vs3
**Then Mary took about a pint of pure nard, an
expensive perfume, she poured it on Jesus feet and
wiped it with her hair....** vs. 7 Jesus replied "Leave her
alone it was intended that she should save this perfume for
the day of my burial" John 12:9 Now a great many of the
Jews knew that He (Jesus) was there; and **they came, not
for Jesus' sake only, but that they might also see
Lazarus, whom He had raised from the dead.** John
12:10 But **the chief priests plotted to put Lazarus to
death also,** John 12:11 because on account of him many
of the Jews went away and **believed in Jesus.**

Preparation for the Feasts of GOD start on the 10th day of the month with the choosing of the Passover lamb, which will be killed on the 14th day of the month and continues through the 22nd day of Nisan, the first month of the year. **The Feasts of GOD** to be celebrated in the first month of the year include Passover, Unleavened Bread, and First Fruits. **The Feast of Unleavened Bread** begins with a High Sabbath on the Fifteenth day of the month and ends with a High Sabbath on the 22nd day. **The reason the Passover is not a High Sabbath is that the lambs are killed by each family and therefore Passover is a day of work.**

Feast "Preparation day number 1" of GOD's Feast
Four days until Passover, Tenth day of the month
<u>Triumphant Entry on the Sabbath</u>

Exodus 12:2 Tell the whole community of Israel that on **the tenth day of the month,** each man is to take a lamb for his family, one for each household…vs. 6 take care of the (lambs) them **until the fourteenth day of the month** when all the people of the community of Israel must slaughter them at twilight…. vs. 8 that night they are to eat the meat roasted over the fire with bitter herbs and bread made without yeast.

6:PM Continuation of the Evening meal and **the beginning of the 10th day of the month**
        John 12:2 there they made Him a supper; and Martha served, but Lazarus was one of those who sat at the table with Him. John 12:3 Then Mary took a pound of very costly oil of spikenard, anointed the feet of Jesus, and wiped His feet with her hair. And the house was filled with the fragrance of the oil. John 12:4 But one of His disciples, Judas Iscariot, Simon's son, who would betray Him, said, John 12:5 "Why was this fragrant oil not sold for three hundred denarii and given to the poor?" John 12:6 this he said, not that he cared for the poor, but because he was a thief, and had the money box; and he used to take what was put in it. John 12:7 But Jesus said "Let her alone; she has kept this for the day of "My" burial. John 12:8 for the poor you have with you always,

but Me you do not have always." Other Gospels indicate this anointing comes two evenings later.

7:PM

8:PM

9:PM

10:PM

11:PM

12:PM   Overnight

1:AM

2:AM

Sabbath a day with no work
not sanctioned by GOD's
Feast Requirements

3:AM

4:AM

5:AM Mark 11:7 Then they brought the colt to Jesus and threw their clothes on it, and He sat on it.

Mark 11:8 And many spread their clothes on the road, and others cut down leafy branches from the trees and spread them on the road. Mark 11:9 Then those who went before and those who followed cried out, saying: "Hosanna!'BLESSED IS HE WHO COMES IN THE NAME OF THE LORD!'

The High Priest and a large group of priests and pilgrims walk over to Bethlehem for the choosing of the Passover Lamb from the sheepfolds of Bethlehem to be paraded through Jerusalem to the praises of the Jewish nation and then kept at the Temple, four days, to await Passover. During the parade, the Psalms 118 sung by the pilgrims there for the Feasts of GOD.

Mark 11:10 Blessed is the kingdom of our father David That comes in the Name of the Lord! Hosanna in the highest!"

6:AM Luke 19:37 Then, **as He was now drawing near the descent of the Mount of Olives,** the whole multitude of the disciples began to rejoice and praise God with a loud voice for all the mighty works they had seen, Luke 19:38 saying: " 'BLESSED IS THE KING WHO COMES IN THE NAME OF THE LORD!' Peace in heaven and glory in the highest!" Luke 19:39 And some of the Pharisees called to Him from the crowd, "Teacher, rebuke Your disciples." Luke 19:40 But He answered and said to them, "I tell you that if these should keep silent, the stones would immediately cry out."

7:AM Luke 19:41 **Now as He drew near, He saw the city and wept over it,** Luke 19:42 saying, "If you had known, even you, especially in this your day, the things that make for your peace! But now they are hidden from your eyes. Luke 19:43 For days will come upon you when your enemies will build an embankment around you, surround you and close you in on every side, Luke 19:44 and level you, and your children within you, to the ground; and they will not leave in you one stone upon another, because you did not know the time of your visitation."

8:AM John; The next day the great crowd that had come for the Feast (Passover, Unleavened Bread and First Fruits) heard that Jesus was on his way to Jerusalem. They took palm branches and went out to meet him, shouting

"Hosanna" "Blessed is he who comes in the name of Lord, Blessed is the King of Israel"

9:AM The Hebrew Nation **had heard of Jesus doing two miracles that no other person had ever done;** the raising of Lazarus from the dead after four days and the healing of a man born blind. And hope was alive wanting this man to be their Messiah come to redeem Israel. The Hebrew pilgrims in Jerusalem were trying to see the "King" they had been anticipating to redeem Israel. Hundreds of thousands if not a million Hebrew pilgrims were in Jerusalem to meet with their GOD and were lined up to welcome the High Priest as he brings the "Passover lamb" through the streets to be staked in the Temple for 4 days until Passover.

10:AM Matt. 21:4, 5 The requisitioning of the animals fulfilled prophecies by Isaiah and Zechariah:

"Tell the daughter of Zion, 'Behold, your King is coming to you, Lowly, and sitting on a donkey, a colt, the foal of a donkey.'"

11:AM

12:AM

1:PM

2:PM

3:PM Mark 11:11 And Jesus went into Jerusalem and into the temple. So when He had looked around at all things, as the hour was already late, He went out to Bethany with the twelve.

4:PM

5:PM The beginning of the evening meal

Dusk ending of the Sabbath and beginning the Calendar day for the 2nd Preparation day for the Feast of GOD

Feast Preparation day number 2
First day of the week

The end of the Triumphal entry and the Sabbath and a day of work in the Jewish culture begins, Judas sets up his betrayal, Jesus cleanses the Temple, teaches, and heals the sick. There were incredible miracles in The Lord's words actions and instructions; for example When the Disciples asked the Lord where he wanted to prepare to have the Passover, He said go into town and find a man carrying a water pot, men did not carry water, and tell him the master needs his upper room, which just happens to be furnished amply for the size of the Lord's group.

6:PM   Night approaches; and the beginning of the 11th day of the month
Luke 22:3   At this point the Adversary went into (Judas)Y'hudah from K'riot, who was one of the Twelve. Luke 22:4 He approached the head cohanim (High Priest) and the Temple guard and discussed with them how he might turn Yeshua (Jesus) over to them. Luke 22:5   They were pleased and offered to pay him money. Luke 22:6 He agreed and began looking for a good opportunity to betray Yeshua (Jesus) without the people's knowledge. (Two days before the Last Supper)
7:PM   Jesus after dinner went to Garden of Gethsemane (Mount of Olives) to pray.
8:PM
9:PM
10:PM
11:PM
12:PM   Overnight

1:AM

2:AM

3:AM

4:AM

5:AM   Mark 11:12 Now the next morning, when they had come out from Bethany, He (Jesus) was hungry. Mark 11:13 And seeing from afar a fig tree having leaves, He went to see if perhaps He would find something on it. When He came to it, He found nothing but leaves, for it was not the season for figs. Mark 11:14 In response Jesus said to it, "Let no one eat fruit from you ever again." And His disciples heard it.

6:AM   Luke 21:37 Yeshua spent his days at the Temple, teaching; while at night he went out and stayed on the hill called the Mount of Olives. Luke 21:38 All the people would rise with the dawn to come and hear him at the Temple courts. Luke 22:1 But the festival of Matzah (Unleavened Bread), known as Pesach (Passover), was approaching; Luke 22:7 Then came ("the Day of" is not in original text) Unleavened Bread, when the Passover must be killed. Luke 22:8

And He sent Peter and John, saying, "Go and prepare the Passover for us, that we may eat." Luke 22:9 So they said to Him, "Where do You want us to prepare?" Luke 22:10 And He said to them, "Behold, when you have entered the city, a man will meet you carrying a pitcher of water; follow him into the house which he enters. Luke 22:11 Then you shall say to the master of the house, 'The Teacher says to you, "Where is the guest room where I may eat the Passover with My disciples?" ' Luke 22:12 Then he will show you a large, furnished upper room; there make ready." Luke 22:13 So they went and found it just as He had said to them, and they prepared the Passover.

7:AM Mark 11:15 So they came to Jerusalem. Then Jesus went into the temple and began to drive out those who bought and sold in the temple, and overturned the tables of the money changers and the seats of those who sold doves. Mark 11:16 And He would not allow anyone to carry wares through the temple. Mark 11:17 Then He taught, saying to them, "Is it not written, 'MY HOUSE SHALL BE CALLED A HOUSE OF PRAYER FOR ALL NATIONS'? But you have made it a 'DEN OF THIEVES.'" Mark 11:18 And the scribes and chief priests heard it and sought how they might destroy Him; for they feared Him, because all the people were astonished at His teaching.

8:AM And as He was walking in the temple, the chief priests, the scribes, and the elders came to Him.

Mark 11:28 And they said to Him, "By what authority are You doing these things? And who gave You this authority to do these things?" Mark 11:29 But Jesus answered and said to them, "I also will ask you one question; then answer Me, and I will tell you by what authority I do these things: Mark 11:30 The baptism of John was it from heaven or from men? Answer Me." Mark 11:31 And they reasoned among themselves, saying, "If we say, 'From heaven,' He will say, 'Why then did you not believe him?' Mark 11:32 But if we say, 'From men' "they feared the people, for all counted John to have been a prophet indeed. Mark 11:33 so they answered and said to Jesus, "We do not know." And Jesus answered and said to them, "Neither will I tell you by what authority I do these things."

9:AM Mat 21:14 Then the blind and the lame came to Him in the temple, and He healed them. Mat 21:15 But when the chief priests and scribes saw the wonderful things that He did, and the children crying out in the temple and saying, "Hosanna to the Son of David!" they were indignant

Mat 21:16 and said to Him, "Do You hear what these are saying?" And Jesus said to them, "Yes. Have you never read, 'OUT OF THE MOUTH OF BABES AND NURSING INFANTS YOU HAVE PERFECTED PRAISE'?"

10:AM

11:AM John 12:42 Nevertheless even among the rulers many believed in Him, but because of the Pharisees they did not confess Him, lest they should be put out of the synagogue; John 12:43 for they loved the praise of men more than the praise of God. John 12:44 Then Jesus cried out and said, "He who believes in Me, believes not in Me but in Him who sent Me. John 12:45 And he who sees Me sees Him who sent Me. John 12:46 I have come as a light into the world, that whoever believes in Me should not abide in darkness. John 12:47 And if anyone hears My words and does not believe, I do not judge him; for I did not come to judge the world but to save the world.

12:AM John 12:48 He who rejects Me, and does not receive My words, has that which judges him— the word that I have spoken will judge him in the last day. John 12:49 For I have not spoken on My own authority; but the Father who sent Me gave Me a command, what I should say and what I should speak. John 12:50 And I know that His command is everlasting life. Therefore, whatever I speak, just as the Father has told Me, so I speak."

1:PM   Look, the world has gone after Him!" John 12:31 Now is the judgment of this world; now the ruler of this world will be cast out. John 12:32 And I, if I am lifted up from the earth, will draw all peoples to Myself." John 12:33 This He said, signifying by what death He would die. John 12:34 The people answered Him, "We have heard from the law that the Christ remains forever; and how can You say, 'The Son of Man must be lifted up'? Who is this Son of Man?" John 12:35 Then Jesus said to them, "A little while longer the light is with you. Walk while you have the light, lest darkness overtake you; he who walks in darkness does not know where he is going. John 12:36 While you have the light, believe in the light, that you may become sons of light." These things **Jesus spoke, and departed, and was hidden from them.** John 12:37 But although He had done so many signs before them, they did not believe in Him, John 12:38 that the word of Isaiah the prophet might be fulfilled, which he spoke: "LORD, WHO HAS BELIEVED OUR REPORT? AND TO WHOM HAS THE ARM OF THE LORD BEEN REVEALED?" John 12:39 Therefore they could not believe, because Isaiah said again: John 12:40 "HE HAS BLINDED THEIR EYES AND HARDENED THEIR HEARTS, LEST THEY SHOULD SEE WITH THEIR EYES, LEST THEY SHOULD UNDERSTAND WITH THEIR HEARTS AND TURN, SO THAT I SHOULD HEAL THEM." John 12:41 These things Isaiah said when he saw His glory and spoke of Him.

2:PM   Mat 22:1 And Jesus answered and spoke to them again by parables and said: Mat 22:2 "The kingdom of heaven is like a certain king who arranged a marriage for his son, Mat 22:3 and sent out his servants to call those who were invited to the wedding; and they were not willing to come.

Mat 22:4 Again, he sent out other servants, saying, 'Tell those who are invited, "See, I have prepared my dinner; my oxen and fatted cattle are killed, and all things are ready. Come to the wedding." 'Mat 22:5 But they made light of it and went their ways, one to his own farm, another to his business. Mat 22:6 And the rest seized his servants, treated them spitefully, and killed them.

Mat 22:7 But when the king heard about it, he was furious. And he sent out his armies, destroyed those murderers, and burned up their city. Mat 22:8 then he said to his servants, 'The wedding is ready, but those who were invited were not worthy. Mat 22:9 Therefore go into the highways, and as many as you find, invite to the wedding.' Mat 22:10 So those servants went out into the highways and gathered together all whom they found, both bad and good. And the wedding hall was filled with guests. Mat 22:33 And when the multitudes heard this, they were astonished at His teaching.

3:PM Mat 23:1 Then Jesus spoke to the multitudes and to His disciples, Mat 23:2 saying: "The scribes and the Pharisees sit in Moses' seat. Mat 23:3 Therefore whatever they tell you to observe, that observe and do, but do not do according to their works; for they say, and do not do. Mat 23:4 For they bind heavy burdens, hard to bear, and lay them on men's shoulders; but they themselves will not move them with one of their fingers. Mat 23:5 But all their works they do to be seen by men. They make their phylacteries broad and enlarge the borders of their garments. Mat 23:6 They love the best places at feasts, the best seats in the synagogues, Mat 23:7 greetings in the marketplaces, and to be called by men, 'Rabbi, Rabbi.' Mat 23:8 But you, do not be called 'Rabbi'; for One is your Teacher, the Christ, and you are all brethren. Mat 23:9 do not call anyone on earth your father; for One is your Father, He who is in heaven. Mat 23:10 And do not be called teachers; for One is your Teacher, the Christ. Mat 23:11 But he who is greatest among you shall be your servant. Mat 23:12 and whoever exalts himself will be humbled, and he who humbles himself will be exalted. Mat 23:13 "But woe to you, scribes and Pharisees, hypocrites! For you shut up the kingdom of heaven against men; for you neither go in yourselves, nor do you allow those who are entering to go in. Mat 23:14 Woe to you, scribes and Pharisees, hypocrites! For you devour widows' houses, and for a pretense make long prayers. Therefore you will receive greater condemnation. Mat 23:15 "Woe to you, scribes and Pharisees, hypocrites! For you travel land and sea to win one proselyte, and when he is won, you make him twice as much a son of hell as yourselves. Mat 23:16 "Woe to you, blind guides, who say, 'Whoever swears by the temple, it is nothing; but whoever swears by the gold of the temple, he is obliged to perform it.' Mat 23:17 Fools and blind! For which is greater, the gold or the temple that sanctifies the gold? Mat 23:18 And, 'Whoever swears by the altar, it is nothing; but whoever swears by the gift that is on it, he is obliged to perform it.' Mat 23:19 Fools and blind! For which is greater, the gift or the altar that sanctifies the gift? Mat 23:20 Therefore he who swears by the altar, swears by it and by all things on it. Mat 23:21 He who swears by the temple, swears by it and by Him who dwells in it. Mat 23:22 And he who swears by heaven, swears by the throne of God and by Him who sits on it.

at 23:23 "Woe to you, scribes and Pharisees, hypocrites! For you pay tithe of mint and anise and cummin, and have neglected the weightier matters of the law: justice and mercy and faith. These you ought to have done, without leaving the others undone. Mat 23:24 Blind guides, who strain out a gnat and swallow a camel! Mat 23:25 "Woe to you, scribes and Pharisees, hypocrites! For you cleanse the outside of the cup and dish, but inside they are full of extortion and self-indulgence. Mat 23:26 Blind Pharisee, first cleanse the inside of the cup and dish, that the outside of them may be clean also. Mat 23:27 "Woe to you, scribes and Pharisees, hypocrites! For you are like whitewashed tombs which indeed appear beautiful outwardly, but inside are full of dead men's bones and all uncleanness. Mat 23:28 Even so you also outwardly appear righteous to men, but inside you are full of hypocrisy and lawlessness. Mat 23:29 "Woe to you, scribes and Pharisees, hypocrites! Because you build the tombs of the prophets and adorn the monuments of the righteous, Mat 23:30 and say, 'If we had lived in the days of our fathers, we would not have been partakers with them in the blood of the prophets.' Mat 23:31 "Therefore you are witnesses against yourselves that you are sons of those who murdered the prophets. Mat 23:32 Fill up, then, the measure of your fathers' guilt. Mat 23:33 Serpents, brood of vipers! How can you escape the condemnation of hell? Mat 23:34 Therefore, indeed, I send you prophets, wise men, and scribes: some of them you will kill and crucify, and some of them you will scourge in your synagogues and persecute from city to city, Mat 23:35 that on you may come all the righteous blood shed on the earth, from the blood of righteous Abel to the blood of Zechariah, son of Berechiah, whom you murdered between the temple and the altar. Mat 23:36 Assuredly, I say to you, all these things will come upon this generation. Mat 23:37 "O Jerusalem, Jerusalem, the one who kills the prophets and stones those who are sent to her! How often I wanted to gather your children together, as a hen gathers her chicks under her wings, but you were not willing! Mat 23:38 See! Your house is left to you desolate; Mat 23:39 for I say to you, you shall see Me no more till you say, 'BLESSED is HE WHO COMES IN THE NAME OF THE LORD!' "

4:PM Mat 24:1 Then Jesus went out and departed from the temple, and His disciples came up to show Him the buildings of the temple. Mat 24:2 And Jesus said to them, "Do you not see all these things? Assuredly, I say to you, not one stone shall be left here upon another, that shall not be thrown down."

Night approaches for the Olivet discourse

Mat 24:3 Now as He sat on the Mount of Olives, the disciples came to Him and of the end of the age?" privately, saying, "Tell us, when will these things be? And what will be the sign of Your coming, Mat 24:4 And Jesus answered and said to them: "Take heed that no one deceives you. Mat 24:5 for many will come in My name, saying, 'I am the Christ,' and will deceive many. Mat 24:6 and you will hear of wars and rumors of wars. See that you are not troubled; for all these things must come to pass, but the end is not yet. Mat 24:7 for nation will rise against nation, and kingdom against kingdom. And there will be famines, pestilences, and earthquakes in various places. Mat 24:8 all these are the beginning of sorrows. Mat 24:9 "Then they will deliver you up to tribulation and kill you, and you will be hated by all nations for my name's sake. Mat 24:10 and then many will be offended, will betray one another, and will hate one another. Mat 24:11 Then many false prophets will rise up and deceive many. Mat 24:12 and because lawlessness will abound, the love of many will grow cold. Mat 24:13 But he who endures to the end shall be saved. Mat 24:14 And this gospel of the kingdom will be preached in all the world as a witness to all the nations, and then the end will come. Mat 24:15 "Therefore when you see the 'ABOMINATION OF DESOLATION,' spoken of by Daniel the prophet, standing in the holy place" (whoever reads, let him understand), Mat 24:16 "then let those who are in Judea flee to the mountains. Mat 24:17 Let him who is on the housetop not go down to take anything out of his house. Mat 24:18 and let him who is in the field not go back to get his clothes. Mat 24:19 But woe to those who are pregnant and to those who are nursing babies in those days! Mat 24:20 And pray that your flight may not be in winter or on the Sabbath. Mat 24:21 For then there will be great tribulation, such as has not been since the beginning of the world until this time, no, nor ever shall be. Mat 24:22 And unless those days were shortened, no flesh would be saved; but for the elect's sake those days will be shortened. Mat 24:23 "Then if anyone says to you, 'Look, here is the Christ!' or 'There!' do not believe it. Mat 24:24 For false christs and false prophets will rise and show great signs and wonders to deceive, if possible, even the elect. Mat 24:25 See, I have told you beforehand. Mat 24:26 "Therefore if they say to you, 'Look, He is in the desert!' do not go out; or 'Look, He is in the inner rooms!' do not believe it. Mat 24:27 For as the lightning comes from the east and flashes to the west, so also will the coming of the Son of Man be. Mat 24:28 For wherever the carcass is, there the eagles will be gathered together. Mat 24:29 "Immediately after the tribulation of those days the sun will be darkened, and the moon will not give its light; the stars will fall from heaven, and the powers of the heavens will be shaken. Mat 24:30 Then the sign of the Son of Man will appear in heaven, and then all the tribes of the earth will mourn, and they will see the Son of Man coming on the clouds of heaven with power and great glory. Mat 24:31 And He will send His angels with a great sound of a trumpet, and they will gather together His elect from the four winds, from one end of heaven to the other. Mat 24:32 "Now learn this parable from the fig tree: When its branch has already become tender and puts forth leaves, you know that summer is near. Mat 24:33 So you also, when you see all these things, know that it is near—at the doors! Mat 24:34 Assuredly, I say to you, this generation will by no means pass away till all these things take place. Mat 24:35 Heaven and earth will pass away, but My words will by no means pass away. Mat 24:36 "But of that day and hour no one knows, not even the angels of heaven, but My Father only. Mat 24:37 But as the days of Noah were, so also will the coming of the Son of Man be. Mat 24:38 For as in the days before the flood, they were eating and drinking, marrying and giving in marriage, until the day that Noah entered the ark, Mat 24:39 and did not know until the flood came and took them all away, so also will the coming of the Son of Man be. Mat 24:40 Then two men will be in the field: one will be taken and the other left. Mat 24:41 Two women will be grinding at the mill: one will be taken and the other left. Mat 24:42 Watch therefore, for you do not know what hour your Lord is coming. Mat 24:43 But know this, that if the master of the house had known what hour the thief would come, he would have watched and not allowed his house to be broken into. Mat 24:44 Therefore you also be ready, for the Son of Man is coming at an hour you do not expect. Mat 24:45 "Who then is a faithful and wise servant, whom his master made ruler over his household, to give them food in due season? Mat 24:46 blessed is that servant whom his master, when he comes, will find so doing. Mat 24:47 Assuredly, I say to you that he will make him ruler over all his goods. Mat 24:48 But if that evil servant says in his heart, 'My master is delaying his coming,' Mat 24:49 and begins to beat his fellow servants, and to eat and drink with the drunkards, Mat 24:50 the master of that servant will come on a day when he is not looking for him and at an hour that he is not aware of, Mat 24:51 and will cut him in two and appoint him his portion with the hypocrites. There shall be weeping and gnashing of teeth.

5:PM   Mat 25:1 "Then the kingdom of heaven shall be likened to ten virgins who took their lamps and went out to meet the bridegroom. Mat 25:2 Now five of them were wise, and five were foolish.

Mat 25:3 Those who were foolish took their lamps and took no oil with them, Mat 25:4 but the wise took oil in their vessels with their lamps. Mat 25:5 but while the bridegroom was delayed, they all slumbered and slept. Mat 25:6 "And at midnight a cry was heard: 'Behold, the bridegroom is coming; go out to meet him!' Mat 25:7 then all those virgins arose and trimmed their lamps.

Mat 25:8 and the foolish said to the wise, 'Give us some of your oil, for our lamps are going out.'

Mat 25:9 But the wise answered, saying, 'No, lest there should not be enough for us and you; but go rather to those who sell, and buy for yourselves.' Mat 25:10 and while they went to buy, the bridegroom came, and those who were ready went in with him to the wedding; and the door was shut. Mat 25:11 "Afterward the other virgins came also, saying, 'Lord, Lord, open to us!' Mat 25:12 But he answered and said, 'Assuredly, I say to you, I do not know you.' Mat 25:13 "Watch therefore, for you know neither the day nor the hour in which the Son of Man is coming. Mat 25:14 "For the kingdom of heaven is like a man traveling to a far country, who called his own servants and delivered his goods to them. Mat 25:15 and to one he gave five talents, to another two, and to another one, to each according to his own ability; and immediately he went on a journey. Mat 25:16 Then he who had received the five talents went and traded with them, and made another five talents. Mat 25:17 And likewise he who had received two gained two more also. Mat 25:18 but he who had received one went and dug in the ground, and hid his lord's money. Mat 25:19 after a long time the lord of those servants came and settled accounts with them. Mat 25:20 "So he who had received five talents came and brought five other talents, saying, 'Lord, you delivered to me five talents; look, I have gained five more talents besides them.'

Mat 25:21 His lord said to him, 'Well done, good and faithful servant; you were faithful over a few things, I will make you ruler over many things. Enter into the joy of your lord.' Mat 25:22 He also who had received two talents came and said, 'Lord, you delivered to me two talents; look, I have gained two more talents besides them.' Mat 25:23 His lord said to him, 'Well done, good and faithful servant; you have been faithful over a few things, I will make you ruler over many things. Enter into the joy of your lord.' Mat 25:24 "Then he who had received the one talent came and said, 'Lord, I knew you to be a hard man, reaping where you have not sown, and gathering where you have not scattered seed. Mat 25:25 And I was afraid, and went and hid your talent in the ground. Look, there you have what is yours.' Mat 25:26 "But his lord answered and said to him, 'You wicked and lazy servant, you knew that I reap where I have not sown, and gather where I have not scattered seed. Mat 25:27 So you ought to have deposited my money with the bankers, and at my coming I would have received back my own with interest. Mat 25:28 So take the talent from him, and give it to him who has ten talents. Mat 25:29 'For to everyone who has, more will be given, and he will have abundance; but from him who does not have, even what he has will be taken away. Mat 25:30 And cast the unprofitable servant into the outer darkness. There will be weeping and gnashing of teeth.' Mat 25:31 "When the Son of Man comes in His glory, and all the holy angels with Him, then He will sit on the throne of His glory. Mat 25:32 All the nations will be gathered before Him, and He will separate them one from another, as a shepherd divides his sheep from the goats. Mat 25:33 And

He will set the sheep on His right hand, but the goats on the left. Mat 25:34 Then the King will say to those on His right hand, 'Come, you blessed of My Father, inherit the kingdom prepared for you from the foundation of the world: Mat 25:35 for I was hungry and you gave Me food; I was thirsty and you gave Me drink; I was a stranger and you took Me in; Mat 25:36 I was naked and you clothed Me; I was sick and you visited Me; I was in prison and you came to Me.' Mat 25:37 "Then the righteous will answer Him, saying, 'Lord, when did we see You hungry and feed You, or thirsty and give You drink? Mat 25:38 When did we see You a stranger and take You in, or naked and clothe You? Mat 25:39 Or when did we see You sick, or in prison, and come to You?' Mat 25:40 And the King will answer and say to them, 'Assuredly, I say to you, inasmuch as you did it to one of the least of these My brethren, you did it to Me.' Mat 25:41 "Then He will also say to those on the left hand, 'Depart from Me, you cursed, into the everlasting fire prepared for the devil and his angels: Mat 25:42 for I was hungry and you gave Me no food; I was thirsty and you gave Me no drink; Mat 25:43 I was a stranger and you did not take Me in, naked and you did not clothe Me, sick and in prison and you did not visit Me.'
Mat 25:44 "Then they also will answer Him, saying, 'Lord, when did we see You hungry or thirsty or a stranger or naked or sick or in prison, and did not minister to You?' Mat 25:45 Then He will answer them, saying, 'Assuredly, I say to you, inasmuch as you did not do it to one of the least of these, you did not do it to Me.' Mat 25:46 And these will go away into everlasting punishment, but the righteous into eternal life." Mat 26:1 Now it came to pass,

when Jesus had finished all these sayings, that He said to His disciples, Mat 26:2 "You know that after two days is the Passover, and the Son of Man will be delivered up to be crucified."

Mat 26:3 Then the chief priests, the scribes, and the elders of the people assembled at the palace of the high priest, who was called Caiaphas, Mat 26:4 and plotted to take Jesus by trickery and kill Him. Mat 26:5 But they said, **"Not during the feast, lest there be an uproar among the people."**

Dusk, the beginning of the Calendar Day for the Third day of Preparation for The Feasts of GOD.

Feast Preparation day number 3
Second day of the week
Another day of preparation for the Jewish households to clean their homes, clothes, persons, Passover lamb, and children to learn questions about the exodus. Jesus Christ is questioning and answering questions about GOD and teaching people at the Temple and the apostles each night at the Mount of Olives.

6:PM   Night approaches and the evening meal continues and **the 12th day of the month begins.**
7:PM   Jesus goes to the Garden of Gethsemane for teaching and prayer
8:PM
9:PM
10:PM
11:PM
12:PM
1:AM   Overnight
2:AM
3:AM
4:AM
5:AM   Mark 11:20 **Now in the morning,** as they passed by, they saw the fig tree dried up from the roots.
Mark 11:21 And Peter, remembering, said to Him, "Rabbi, look! The fig tree which You cursed has withered away."
Mark 11:22 So Jesus answered and said to them, "Have faith in God. Mark 11:23 For assuredly, I say to you,

whoever says to this mountain, 'Be removed and be cast into the sea,' and does not doubt in his heart, but believes that those things he says will be done, he will have whatever he says. Mark 11:24 Therefore I say to you, whatever things you ask when you pray, believe that you receive them, and you will have them. Mark 11:25 "And whenever you stand praying, if you have anything against anyone, forgive him, that your Father in heaven may also forgive you your trespasses. Mark 11:26 but if you do not forgive, neither will your Father in heaven forgive your trespasses."

6:AM   Luke 21:37 Yeshua spent his days at the Temple, teaching; while at night he went out and stayed on the hill called the Mount of Olives. Luke 21:38 All **the people would rise with the dawn** to come and hear him at the Temple courts. Luke 22:1 But the festival of Matzah (Unleavened Bread), known as Pesach (Passover), was approaching;

7:AM   Mark 12:1 Then He began to speak to them in parables: "A man planted a vineyard and set a hedge around it, dug a place for the wine vat and built a tower. And he leased it to vinedressers and went into a far country. Mark 12:2 now at vintage-time he sent a servant to the vinedressers, that he might receive some of the fruit of the vineyard from the vinedressers. Mark 12:3 and they took him and beat him and sent him away empty-handed. Mark 12:4 again he sent them another servant, and at him they threw stones, wounded him in the head, and sent him away shamefully treated. Mark 12:5 and again he sent another, and him they killed; and many others, beating some and killing some. Mark 12:6 Therefore still having one son, his beloved, he also sent him to them last, saying, 'They will respect my son.' Mark 12:7 But those vinedressers said among themselves, 'This is the heir. Come, let us kill him, and the inheritance will be ours.' Mark 12:8 So they took him and killed him and cast him out of the vineyard. Mark 12:9 "Therefore what will the owner of the vineyard do? He will come and destroy the vinedressers, and give the vineyard to others.

8:AM Mark 12:10 Have you not even read this Scripture: 'THE STONE WHICH THE BUILDERS REJECTED HAS BECOME THE CHIEF CORNERSTONE. Mark 12:11 THIS WAS THE LORD'S DOING, AND IT IS MARVELOUS IN OUR EYES'?" Mark 12:12 **And they sought to lay hands on Him, but feared the multitude,** for they knew He had spoken the parable against them. So they left Him and went away. Mat 22:1 And Jesus answered and spoke to them again by parables and said: Mat 22:2 "The kingdom of heaven is like a certain king who arranged a marriage for his son, Mat 22:3 and sent out his servants to call those who were invited to the wedding; and they were not willing to come. Mat 22:4 Again, he sent out other servants, saying, 'Tell those who are invited, "See, I have prepared my dinner; my oxen and fatted cattle are killed, and all things are ready. Come to the wedding." ' Mat 22:5 But they made light of it and went their ways, one to his own farm, another to his business. Mat 22:6 And the rest seized his servants, treated them spitefully, and killed them. Mat 22:7 But when the king heard about it, he was furious. And he sent out his armies, destroyed those murderers, and burned up their city.

Mat 22:8 then he said to his servants, 'The wedding is

ready, but those who were invited were not worthy. Mat 22:9 Therefore go into the highways, and as many as you find, invite to the wedding.' Mat 22:10 So those servants went out into the highways and gathered together all whom they found, both bad and good. And the wedding hall was filled with guests. Mat 22:11 "But when the king came in to see the guests, he saw a man there who did not have on a wedding garment. Mat 22:12 So he said to him, 'Friend, how did you come in here without a wedding garment?' And he was speechless. Mat 22:13 Then the king said to the servants, 'Bind him hand and foot, take him away, and cast him into outer darkness; there will be weeping and gnashing of teeth.' Mat 22:14 "For many are called, but few are chosen." Mat 22:15 **Then the Pharisees went and plotted how they might entangle Him in His talk. Mat 22:16**

9:AM Mar 12:13 **Then they sent to Jesus some of the Pharisees and the Herodians, to catch (Jesus) Him in His words.** Mark 12:14 When they had come, they said to Him, "Teacher, we know that You are true, and care about no one; for You do not regard the person of men, but teach the way of God in truth. Is it lawful to pay taxes to Caesar, or not? Mark 12:15 Shall we pay, or shall we not pay?" But He, knowing their hypocrisy, said to them, "Why do you test Me? Bring Me a denarius that I may see it." Mark 12:16 So they brought it. And He said to them, "Whose image and inscription is this?" They said to Him, "Caesar's." Mark 12:17 And Jesus answered and said to them, "Render to Caesar the things that are Caesar's, and to God the things that are God's." And they marveled at Him. **10:AM** Mark 12:18 **Then some Sadducees, who say**

there is no resurrection, came to (Jesus) Him; and they asked Him, saying: Mark 12:19 "Teacher, Moses wrote to us that if a man's brother dies, and leaves his wife behind, and leaves no children, his brother should take his wife and raise up offspring for his brother. Mark 12:20 now there were seven brothers. The first took a wife; and dying, he left no offspring. Mark 12:21 And the second took her, and he died; nor did he leave any offspring. And the third likewise. Mark 12:22 So the seven had her and left no offspring. Last of all the woman died also. Mark 12:23 Therefore, in the resurrection, when they rise, whose wife will she be? For all seven had her as wife." Mark 12:24 Jesus answered and said to them, "Are you not therefore mistaken, because you do not know the Scriptures nor the power of God? Mark 12:25 For when they rise from the dead, they neither marry nor are given in marriage, but are like angels in heaven. Mark 12:26 But concerning the dead, that they rise, have you not read in the book of Moses, in the burning bush passage, how God spoke to him, saying, 'I AM THE GOD OF ABRAHAM, THE GOD OF ISAAC, AND THE GOD OF JACOB' ? Mark 12:27 **He is not the God of the dead, but the God of the living.** You are therefore greatly mistaken." Mark 12:28 Then one of the scribes came, and having heard them reasoning together, perceiving that He had answered them well, asked Him, "Which is the first commandment of all?" Mark 12:29 Jesus answered him, "The first of all the commandments is: 'HEAR, O ISRAEL, THE LORD OUR GOD, THE LORD IS ONE.
11:AM Mark 12:30 AND YOU SHALL LOVE THE LORD YOUR GOD WITH ALL YOUR HEART, WITH

ALL YOUR SOUL, WITH ALL YOUR MIND, AND WITH ALL YOUR STRENGTH.' This is the first commandment. Mark 12:31 And the second, like it, is this: 'YOU SHALL LOVE YOUR NEIGHBOR AS YOURSELF.' There is no other commandment greater than these."

Mar 12:32 So the scribe said to Him, "Well said, Teacher. You have spoken the truth, for there is one God, and there is no other but He. Mark 12:33 And to love Him with all the heart, with all the understanding, with all the soul, and with all the strength, and to love one's neighbor as oneself, is more than all the whole burnt offerings and sacrifices." Mark 12:34 Now when Jesus saw that he answered wisely, He said to him, "You are not far from the kingdom of God." But after that no one dared question Him. Mark 12:35 Then Jesus answered and said, while He taught in the temple, "How is it that the scribes say that the Christ is the Son of David? Mark 12:36 For David himself said by the Holy Spirit: 'THE LORD SAID TO MY LORD, "SIT AT MY RIGHT HAND, TILL I MAKE YOUR ENEMIES YOUR FOOTSTOOL." ' Mark 12:37 Therefore David himself calls Him 'LORD'; how is He then his Son?" **And the common people heard Him gladly.**

12:AM Mat 23:1 Then Jesus spoke to the multitudes and to His disciples, Mat 23:2 saying: "The scribes and the Pharisees sit in Moses' seat. Mat 23:3 Therefore whatever they tell you to observe, that observe and do, but do not do according to their works; for they say, and do not do. Mat 23:4 For they bind heavy burdens, hard to bear, and lay them on men's shoulders; but they themselves will not move them with one of their fingers. Mat 23:5 But all their works they do to be seen by men. They make their phylacteries broad and enlarge the borders of their garments. Mat 23:6 They love the best places at feasts, the best seats in the synagogues, Mat 23:7 greetings in the marketplaces, and to be called by men, 'Rabbi, Rabbi.' Mat 23:8 But you, do not be called 'Rabbi'; for One is your Teacher, the Christ, and you are all brethren. Mat 23:9 Do not call anyone on earth your father; for One is your Father, He who is in heaven. Mat 23:10 And do not be called teachers; for One is your Teacher, the Christ. Mat 23:11 But he who is greatest among you shall be your servant. Mat 23:12 And whoever exalts himself will be humbled, and he who humbles himself will be exalted. Mat 23:13 "But woe to you, scribes and Pharisees, hypocrites! For you shut up the kingdom of heaven against men; for you neither go in yourselves, nor do you allow those who are entering to go in. Mat 23:14 Woe to you, scribes and Pharisees, hypocrites! For you devour widows' houses, and for a pretense make long prayers. Therefore you will receive greater condemnation. Mat 23:15 "Woe to you, scribes and Pharisees, hypocrites! For you travel land and sea to win one proselyte, and when he is won, you make him twice as much a son of hell as yourselves. Mat 23:16 "Woe to you, blind guides, who say, 'Whoever swears by the temple, it is nothing; but whoever swears by the gold of the temple, he is obliged to perform it.' Mat 23:17 Fools and blind! For which is greater, the gold or the temple that sanctifies the gold? Mat 23:18 And, 'Whoever swears by the altar, it is nothing; but whoever swears by the gift that is on it, he is obliged to perform it.' Mat 23:19 Fools and blind! For which is greater, the gift or the altar that sanctifies the gift? Mat 23:20 Therefore he who swears by the altar, swears by it and by all things on it. Mat 23:21 He who swears by the temple, swears by it and by Him who dwells in it. Mat 23:22 And he who swears by heaven, swears by the throne of God and by Him who sits on it.

1:PM Mat 23:23 "Woe to you, scribes and Pharisees, hypocrites! For you pay tithe of mint and anise and cummin, and have neglected the weightier matters of the law: justice and mercy and faith. These you ought to have done, without leaving the others undone. Mat 23:24 Blind guides, who strain out a gnat and swallow a camel! Mat 23:25 "Woe to you, scribes and Pharisees, hypocrites! For you cleanse the outside of the cup and dish, but inside they are full of extortion and self-indulgence. Mat 23:26 Blind Pharisee, first cleanse the inside of the cup and dish, that the outside of them may be clean also. Mat 23:27 "Woe to you, scribes and Pharisees, hypocrites! For you are like whitewashed tombs which indeed appear beautiful outwardly, but inside are full of dead men's bones and all uncleanness. Mat 23:28 Even so you also outwardly appear righteous to men, but inside you are full of hypocrisy and lawlessness. Mat 23:29 "Woe to you, scribes and Pharisees, hypocrites! Because you build the tombs of the prophets and adorn the monuments of the righteous, Mat 23:30 and say, 'If we had lived in the days of our fathers, we would not have been partakers with them in the blood of the prophets.' Mat 23:31 "Therefore you are witnesses against yourselves that you are sons of those who murdered the prophets. Mat 23:32 Fill up, then, the measure of your fathers' guilt. Mat 23:33 Serpents, brood of vipers! How can you escape the condemnation of hell? Mat 23:34

Therefore, indeed, I send you prophets, wise men, and scribes: some of them you will kill and crucify, and some of them you will scourge in your synagogues and persecute from city to city, Mat 23:35 that on you may come all the righteous blood shed on the earth, from the blood of righteous Abel to the blood of Zechariah, son of Berechiah, whom you murdered between the temple and the altar. Mat 23:36 Assuredly, I say to you, all these things will come upon this generation. Mat 23:37 "O Jerusalem, Jerusalem, the one who kills the prophets and stones those who are sent to her! How often I wanted to gather your children together, as a hen gathers her chicks under her wings, but you were not willing! Mat 23:38 See! Your house is left to you desolate; Mat 23:39 for I say to you, you shall see Me no more till you say, 'BLESSED is HE WHO COMES IN THE NAME OF THE LORD!' "

2:PM

3:PM   Mark 12:38 Then He said to them in His teaching (probably teaching to the disciples and pilgrims only), "Beware of the scribes, who desire to go around in long robes, love greetings in the marketplaces, Mark 12:39 the best seats in the synagogues, and the best places at feasts, Mark 12:40 who devour widows' houses, and for a pretense make long prayers. These will receive greater condemnation." Mark 12:41 Now Jesus sat opposite the treasury and saw how the people put money into the treasury. And many who were rich put in much. Mark 12:42 Then one poor widow came and threw in two mites, which make a quadrans. Mark 12:43 So He called His disciples to Himself and said to them, "Assuredly, I say to you that this poor widow has put in more than all those who have given to the treasury; Mark 12:44 for they all put in out of their abundance, but she out of her poverty put in all that she had, her whole livelihood."

4:PM   Mark 13:1 Then as He went out of the temple, one of His disciples said to Him, "Teacher, see what manner of stones and what buildings are here!" Mark 13:2 And Jesus answered and said to him, "Do you see these great buildings? Not one stone shall be left upon another that shall not be thrown down." Mark 13:3 Now as He sat on the Mount of Olives opposite the temple, Peter, James, John, and Andrew asked Him privately, Mark 13:4 "Tell us, when will these things be? And what will be the sign when all these things will be fulfilled?" Mark 13:5 And Jesus, answering them, began to say: "Take heed that no one deceives you. Mark 13:6 For many will come in My name, saying, 'I am He,' and will deceive many. Mark 13:7 But when you hear of wars and rumors of wars, do not be troubled; for such things must happen, but the end is not yet. Mark 13:8 For nation will rise against nation, and kingdom against kingdom. And there will be earthquakes in various places, and there will be famines and troubles. These are the beginnings of sorrows. Mark 13:9 "But watch out for yourselves, for they will deliver you up to councils, and you will be beaten in the synagogues. You will be brought before rulers and kings for My sake, for a testimony to them. Mark 13:10 And the gospel must first be preached to all the nations.

5:PM   This dinner in this scripture is in the Gospels indicating two different times.

Mark 14:3 And being in Bethany at the house of Simon the leper, as He sat at the table, a woman came having an alabaster flask of very costly oil of spikenard. Then she broke the flask and poured it on His head. Mark 14:4 But there were some who were indignant among themselves, and said, "Why was this fragrant oil wasted? Mark 14:5 For it might have been sold for more than three hundred denarii and given to the poor." And they criticized her sharply. Mark 14:6 But Jesus said, "Let her alone. Why do you trouble her? She has done a good work for Me. Mark 14:7 For you have the poor with you always, and whenever you wish you may do them good; but Me you do not have always. Mark 14:8 She has done what she could. **She has come beforehand to anoint My body for burial.** Mark 14:9 Assuredly, I say to you, wherever this gospel is preached in the whole world, what this woman has done will also be told as a memorial to her."

Feast Preparation day number 4
Third day of the week

This day will end with "The Last Supper", but gets started with GOD speaking audibly and praising his son while a large crowd was gathered in the Temple.

6:PM Night approaches and the evening meal continues and **the 13th day of the month begins.**

7:PM Jesus and disciples walk to the Garden of Gethsemane for prayer, praise, and fellowship.

8:PM

9:PM

10:PM

11:PM

12:PM   Overnight

1:AM

2:AM

3:AM

4:AM

5:AM

6:AM Luke 21:37 Yeshua spent his **days at the Temple, teaching; while at night** he went out and stayed on the hill called the Mount of Olives. Luke 21:38 All the people would **rise with the dawn** to come and hear him at the Temple courts. Luke 22:1 But the festival of Matzah (Unleavened Bread), known as Pesach (Passover), was approaching;

7:AM

8:AM John 12:20 Now there were certain Greeks among those who came up to worship at the feast. John 12:21 Then they came to Philip, who was from Bethsaida of Galilee, and asked him, saying, "Sir, we wish to see Jesus."

The Passion of the Christ, 95

John 12:22 Philip came and told Andrew, and in turn Andrew and Philip told Jesus. John 12:23 But Jesus answered them, saying, "The hour has come that the Son of Man should be glorified. John 12:24 Most assuredly, I say to you, unless a grain of wheat falls into the ground and dies, it remains alone; but if it dies, it produces much grain. John 12:25 He who loves his life will lose it, and he who hates his life in this world will keep it for eternal life. John 12:26 If anyone serves Me, let him follow Me; and where I am, there My servant will be also. If anyone serves Me, him My Father will honor. John 12:27 **"Now My soul is troubled, and what shall I say? 'Father, save Me from this hour'? But for this purpose I came to this hour.** John 12:28 Father, glorify Your name." Then a voice came from heaven, saying, "I have both glorified it and will glorify it again." John 12:29 Therefore the people who stood by and heard it said that it had thundered. Others said, "An angel has spoken to Him." John 12:30 Jesus answered and said, "This voice did not come because of Me, but for your sake. John 12:31 Now is the judgment of this world; now the ruler of this world will be cast out.

9:AM
10:AM
11:AM
12:AM
1:PM
2:PM
3:PM
4:PM   The last Supper, __cannot be the Passover meal,__ because it was the day of preparation, and many additional reasons; The Lord served leavened Bread, no mention of

roasting the Sacrificed Family Passover Lamb, bitters, unleavened bread, and when Judas left the dinner, the disciples thought he was going to buy something for the feast. After the Passover Meal it is a High Sabbath and you can't buy anything.

5:PM John 13:1 Now before the Feast of the Passover, when Jesus knew that His hour had come that He should depart from this world to the Father, having loved His own who were in the world, He loved them to the end. John 13:2 And supper being ended, the devil having already put it into the heart of Judas Iscariot, Simon's son, to betray Him, John 13:3 **Jesus, knowing that the Father had given all things into His hands, and that He had come from God and was going to God,**

He sat down, and the twelve apostles with Him. Luke 22:15 Then He said to them, "With fervent desire I have desired to eat this Passover with you before I suffer;

Luke 22:16 for I say to you, **I will no longer eat of it until it is fulfilled in the kingdom of God."** Luke 22:17 Then He took the cup, and gave thanks, and said, "Take this and divide it among yourselves; Luke 22:18 for I say to you, I will not drink of the fruit of the vine until the kingdom of God comes." Luke 22:19 And He took bread (artos leavened bread), gave thanks and broke it, and gave it to them, saying, "This is My body which is given for you; do this in remembrance of Me." Luke 22:20 Likewise He also took the cup after supper, saying, "This cup is the new covenant in My blood, which is shed for you. Luke 22:21 But behold, the hand of My betrayer is with Me on the table. Luke 22:22 And truly the Son of Man goes as it has been determined, but woe to that man by whom He is betrayed!" Luke 22:23 Then they began to question among themselves, which of them it was who would do this thing.

End of the 3rd day of the week according to Jewish Calendar.

Beginning of the Calendar Day when the Passover Lambs will be sacrificed.

Passover
The fourth day of the week
The day the Passover Lambs are killed

The Last Supper is blending into the night and day the Passover lamb is sacrificed. Passover started at sundown the night of the thirteenth and ends with the **death and burial of Jesus Christ** at the twilight of the 14th day of Nisan along with the sacrifice of the Passover lambs for each family.

During this night and early morning the Lord will be arrested and subjected to 2 Jewish Trials and 3 Roman trials. At Twilight The Lord will give up his life and be buried by Joseph of Arimathea and Nichodemus.

The evening meal will be after each family sacrifices their lamb, at twilight on the 14th day of Nisan, and the families will eat the lamb with bitter herbs and unleavened bread Ex 12:2. This meal starts at the end of the Passover day and ends well into the **High Sabbath of Unleavened bread** and Jehovah is praised for his deliverance of the Jewish people from Egypt. Ex 12:16.

6:PM   Judas leaves Last Supper as <u>the beginning of the 14th day of the month begins.</u>

Luke 22:24 Now there was also a dispute among them, as to which of them should be considered the greatest. Luke 22:25 And He (Jesus) said to them, "The kings of the Gentiles exercise lordship over them, and those who exercise authority over them are called 'benefactors.' Luke 22:26 But not so among you; on the contrary, he who is greatest among you, let him be as the younger, and he who governs as he who serves. Luke 22:27 For who is greater, he who sits at the table, or he who serves? Is it not he who sits at the table? Yet I am among you as the One who serves. Luke 22:28 "But you are those who have continued with Me in My trials. Luke 22:29 **And I bestow upon you a kingdom, just as My Father bestowed one upon Me, Luke 22:30 that you may eat and drink at My table in My kingdom, and sit on thrones judging the twelve tribes of Israel."**

Luke 22:31 And the Lord said, "Simon, Simon! Indeed, Satan has asked for you, that he may sift you as wheat. Luke 22:32 But I have prayed for you, that your faith should not fail; and when you have returned to Me, strengthen your brethren." Luke 22:33 But he said to Him, "Lord, I am ready to go with You, both to prison and to death." Luke 22:34 Then He said, "I tell you, Peter, the rooster shall not crow this day before you will deny three times that you know Me." Luke 22:35 And He said to them, "When I sent you without money bag, knapsack, and sandals, did you lack anything?" So they said, "Nothing." Luke 22:36 Then He said to them, "But now, he who has a money bag, let him take it, and likewise a knapsack; and he who has no sword, let him sell his garment and buy one. Luke 22:37 For I say to you that this which is written must still be accomplished in Me: 'AND HE WAS NUMBERED WITH THE TRANSGRESSORS.' For the things concerning Me have an end." Luke 22:38 So they said, "Lord, look, here are two swords." And He said to them, "It is enough." Luke 22:39 Coming out, He went to the Mount of Olives, as He was accustomed, and His disciples also followed Him.

7:PM   John 14:1 "Let not your heart be troubled; you believe in God, believe also in Me. John 14:2 In My Father's house are many mansions; if it were not so, I would have told you. I go to prepare a place for you. John 14:3 And if I go and prepare a place for you, I will come again and receive you to Myself; that where I am, there you may be also. John 14:4 And where I go you know, and the way you know." John 14:5 Thomas said to Him, "Lord, we do not know where You are going, and how can we know the way?" John 14:6 Jesus said to him, "I am the way, the truth, and the life. No one comes to the Father except through Me. John 14:7 "If you had known Me, you would have known My Father also; and from now on you know Him and have seen Him." John 14:8 Philip said to Him, "Lord, show us the Father, and it is sufficient for us." John 14:9 Jesus said to him, "Have I been with you so long, and yet you have not known Me, Philip? He who has seen Me has seen the Father; so how can you say, 'Show us the Father'? John 14:10 Do you not believe that I am in the Father, and the Father in Me? The words that I speak to you I do not speak on My own authority; but the Father who dwells in Me does the works. John 14:11 Believe Me that I am in the Father and the Father in Me, or else believe Me for the sake of the works themselves. John 14:12 "Most assuredly, I say to you, he who believes in Me, the works that I do he will do also; and greater works than these he will do, because I go to My Father. John 14:13 And whatever you ask in My name, that I will do, that the Father may be glorified in the Son. John 14:14 If you ask anything in My name, I will do it. John 14:15 "If you love Me, keep

My commandments. John 14:16 And I will pray the Father, and He will give you another Helper, that He may abide with you forever— John 14:17 the Spirit of truth, whom the world cannot receive, because it neither sees Him nor knows Him; but you know Him, for He dwells with you and will be in you. John 14:18 I will not leave you orphans; I will come to you. John 14:19 "A little while longer and the world will see Me no more, but you will see Me. Because I live, you will live also. John 14:20 At that day you will know that I am in My Father, and you in Me, and I in you. John 14:21 He who has My commandments and keeps them, it is he who loves Me. And he who loves Me will be loved by My Father, and I will love him and manifest Myself to him." John 14:22 Judas (not Iscariot) said to Him, "Lord, how is it that You will manifest Yourself to us, and not to the world?" John 14:23 Jesus answered and said to him, "If anyone loves Me, he will keep My word; and My Father will love him, and We will come to him and make Our home with him. John 14:24 He who does not love Me does not keep My words; and the word which you hear is not Mine but the Father's who sent Me. John 14:25 "These things I have spoken to you while being present with you. John 14:26 But the Helper, the Holy Spirit, whom the Father will send in My name, He will teach you all things, and bring to your remembrance all things that I said to you. John 14:27 Peace I leave with you, My peace I give to you; not as the world gives do I give to you. Let not your heart be troubled, neither let it be afraid. John 14:28 You have heard Me say to you, 'I am going away and coming back to you.' If you loved Me, you would rejoice because I said, 'I am going to the Father,' for My

Father is greater than I. John 14:29 "And now I have told you before it comes, that when it does come to pass, you may believe. John 14:30 I will no longer talk much with you, for the ruler of this world is coming, and he has nothing in Me. John 14:31 But that the world may know that I love the Father, and as the Father gave Me commandment, so I do. Arise, let us go from here.

8:PM Jesus teaching John 15:1 "I am the true vine, and My Father is the vinedresser. John 15:2 Every branch in Me that does not bear fruit He takes away; and every branch that bears fruit He prunes, that it may bear more fruit. John 15:3 You are already clean because of the word which I have spoken to you. John 15:4 Abide in Me, and I in you. As the branch cannot bear fruit of itself, unless it abides in the vine, neither can you, unless you abide in Me. John 15:5 "I am the vine, you are the branches. He who abides in Me, and I in him, bears much fruit; for without Me you can do nothing. John 15:6 If anyone does not abide in Me, he is cast out as a branch and is withered; and they gather them and throw them into the fire, and they are burned. John 15:7 If you abide in Me, and My words abide in you, you will ask what you desire, and it shall be done for you. John 15:8 By this My Father is glorified, that you bear much fruit; so you will be My disciples. John 15:9 "As the Father loved Me, I also have loved you; abide in My love. John 15:10 If you keep My commandments, you will abide in My love, just as I have kept My Father's commandments and abide in His love. John 15:11 "These things I have spoken to you, that My joy may remain in you, and that your joy may be full. John 15:12 This is My commandment, that you love one another as I have loved you. John 15:13 Greater love has no one than this, than to lay down one's life for his friends. John 15:14 You are My friends if you do whatever I command you. John 15:15 No longer do I call you servants, for a servant does not know what his master is doing; but I have called you friends, for all things that I heard from My Father I have made known to you. John 15:16 You did not choose Me, but I chose you and appointed you that you should go and bear fruit, and that your fruit should remain, that whatever you ask the Father in My name He may give you. John 15:17 These things I command you, that you love one another. John 15:18 "If the world hates you, you know that it hated Me before it hated you. John 15:19 If you were of the world, the world would love its own. Yet because you are not of the world, but I chose you out of the world, therefore the world hates you. John 15:20 Remember the word that I said to you, 'A servant is not greater than his master.' If they persecuted Me, they will also persecute you. If they kept My word, they will keep yours also. John 15:21 But all these things they will do to you for My name's sake, because they do not know Him who sent Me. John 15:22 If I had not come and spoken to them, they would have no sin, but now they have no excuse for their sin. John 15:23 He who hates Me hates My Father also. John 15:24 If I had not done among them the works which no one else did, they would have no sin; but now they have seen and also hated both Me and My Father. John 15:25 But this happened that the word might be fulfilled which is written in their law, 'THEY HATED ME WITHOUT A CAUSE.' John 15:26 "But when the Helper comes, whom I shall send to you from the Father, the Spirit of truth who proceeds from the Father, He will testify of Me. John 15:27 And you also will bear witness, because you have been with Me from the beginning.

John 16:1 "These things I have spoken to you, that you should not be made to stumble. John 16:2 They will put you out of the synagogues; yes, the time is coming that whoever kills you will think that he offers God service. John 16:3 And these things they will do to you because they have not known the Father nor Me. John 16:4 But these things I have told you, that when the time comes, you may remember that I told you of them. "And these things I did not say to you at the beginning, because I was with you. John 16:5 "But now I go away to Him who sent Me, and none of you asks Me, 'Where are You going?' John 16:6 But because I have said these things to you, sorrow has filled your heart. John 16:7 Nevertheless I tell you the truth. It is to your advantage that I go away; for if I do not go away, the Helper will not come to you; but if I depart, I will send Him to you.

John 16:8 And when He has come, He will convict the world of sin, and of righteousness, and of judgment: John 16:9 of sin, because they do not believe in Me; John 16:10 of righteousness, because I go to My Father and you see Me no more; John 16:11 of judgment, because the ruler of this world is judged. John 16:12 "I still have many things to say to you, but you cannot bear them now. John 16:13 However, when He, the Spirit of truth, has come, He will guide you into all truth; for He will not speak on His own authority, but whatever He hears He will speak; and He will tell you things to come. John 16:14 He will glorify Me, for He will take of what is Mine and declare it to you.

The Passion of the Christ, 105

John 16:15 All things that the Father has are Mine. Therefore I said that He will take of Mine and declare it to you. John 16:16 "A little while, and you will not see Me; and again a little while, and you will see Me, because I go to the Father." John 16:17 Then some of His disciples said among themselves, "What is this that He says to us, 'A little while, and you will not see Me; and again a little while, and you will see Me'; and, 'because I go to the Father'?" John 16:18 They said therefore, "What is this that He says, 'A little while'? We do not know what He is saying." John 16:19 Now Jesus knew that they desired to ask Him, and He said to them, "Are you inquiring among yourselves about what I said, 'A little while, and you will not see Me; and again a little while, and you will see Me'? John 16:20 Most assuredly, I say to you that you will weep and lament, but the world will rejoice; and you will be sorrowful, but your sorrow will be turned into joy. John 16:21 A woman, when she is in labor, has sorrow because her hour has come; but as soon as she has given birth to the child, she no longer remembers the anguish, for joy that a human being has been born into the world. John 16:22 Therefore you now have sorrow; but I will see you again and your heart will rejoice, and your joy no one will take from you. John 16:23 "And in that day you will ask Me nothing. Most assuredly, I say to you, whatever you ask the Father in My name He will give you. John 16:24 Until now you have asked nothing in My name. Ask, and you will receive, that your joy may be full. John 16:25 "These things I have spoken to you in figurative language; but the time is coming when I will no longer speak to you in figurative language, but I will tell you plainly about the Father. John

The Passion of the Christ, 106

16:26 In that day you will ask in My name, and I do not say to you that I shall pray the Father for you; John 16:27 for the Father Himself loves you, because you have loved Me, and have believed that I came forth from God. John 16:28 I came forth from the Father and have come into the world. Again, I leave the world and go to the Father." John 16:29 His disciples said to Him, "See, now You are speaking plainly, and using no figure of speech! John 16:30 Now we are sure that You know all things, and have no need that anyone should question You. By this we believe that You came forth from God." John 16:31 Jesus answered them, "Do you now believe? John 16:32 Indeed the hour is coming, yes, has now come, that you will be scattered, each to his own, and will leave Me alone. And yet I am not alone, because the Father is with Me. John 16:33 These things I have spoken to you, that in Me you may have peace. In the world you will have tribulation; but be of good cheer, I have overcome the world."

9:PM Mat 26:36 **Then Jesus came with them to a place called Gethsemane,** and said to the disciples, "Sit here while I go and pray over there." Mat 26:37 And He took with Him Peter and the two sons of Zebedee, and He began to be sorrowful and deeply distressed. Mat 26:38 Then He said to them, "My soul is exceedingly sorrowful, even to death. Stay here and watch with Me." Mat 26:39 He went a little farther and fell on His face, and prayed, saying, **"O My Father, if it is possible, let this cup pass from Me; Nevertheless, not as I will, but as You will." John 17:1 Jesus spoke these words, lifted up His eyes to heaven, and said: "Father, the hour has come. Glorify Your Son, that Your Son also may glorify You, John**

17:2 as You have given Him authority over all flesh, that He should give eternal life to as many as You have given Him. John 17:3 And this is eternal life, that they may know You, the only true God, and Jesus Christ whom You have sent. John 17:4 I have glorified You on the earth. I have finished the work which You have given Me to do. John 17:5 And now, O Father, glorify Me together with Yourself, with the glory which I had with You before the world was. John 17:6 "I have manifested Your name to the men whom You have given Me out of the world. They were Yours, You gave them to Me, and they have kept Your word. John 17:7 Now they have known that all things which You have given Me are from You. John 17:8 For I have given to them the words which You have given Me; and they have received them, and have known surely that I came forth from You; and they have believed that You sent Me. John 17:9 "I pray for them. I do not pray for the world but for those whom You have given Me, for they are Yours. John 17:10 And all Mine are Yours, and Yours are Mine, and I am glorified in them. John 17:11 Now I am no longer in the world, but these are in the world, and I come to You. Holy Father, keep through Your name those whom You have given Me, that they may be one as We are. John 17:12 While I was with them in the world, I kept them in Your name. Those whom You gave Me I have kept; and none of them is lost except the son of perdition, that the Scripture might be fulfilled. John 17:13 But now I come to You, and these things I speak in the world, that they may have My joy fulfilled in themselves. John 17:14 I have given them Your word; and the world has hated them because they are not of the world, just as I am not of the world. John 17:15 I do not pray that You should take them out of the world, but that You should keep them from the evil one. John 17:16 They are not of the world, just as I am not of the world. John 17:17 Sanctify them by Your truth. Your word is truth. John 17:18 As You sent Me into the world, I also have sent them into the world. John 17:19 And for their sakes I sanctify Myself, that they also may be sanctified by the truth. John 17:20 "I do not pray for these alone, but also for those who will believe in Me through their word; John 17:21 that they all may be one, as You, Father, are in Me, and I in You; that they also may be one in Us, that the world may believe that You sent Me. John 17:22 And the glory which You gave Me I have given them, that they may be one just as We are one: John 17:23 I in them, and You in Me; that they may be made perfect in one, and that the world may know that You have sent Me, and have loved them as You have loved Me. John 17:24 "Father, I desire that they also whom You gave Me may be with Me where I am, that they may behold My glory which You have given Me; for You loved Me before the foundation of the world. John 17:25 O righteous Father! The world has not known You, but I have known You; and these have known that You sent Me. John 17:26 And I have declared to them Your name, and will declare it, that the love with which You loved Me may be in them, and I in them."

Mat 26:40 Then He came to the disciples and found them sleeping, and said to Peter, "What! Could you not watch with Me one hour? Mat 26:41 Watch and pray, lest you enter into temptation. The spirit indeed is willing, but the flesh is weak." Mat 26:42 Again, a second time, He went away and prayed, saying, "O My Father, if this cup cannot pass away from Me unless I drink it, Your will be done." Mat 26:43 And He came and found them asleep again, for their eyes were heavy. Luke 22:43 There appeared to him an angel from heaven giving him strength,

Luke 22:44 and in great anguish he prayed more intensely, so that his sweat became like drops of blood falling to the ground. Mat 26:44 So He left them, went away again, and prayed the third time, saying the same words. Mat 26:45 Then He came to His disciples and said to them, "Are you still sleeping and resting? Behold, the hour is at hand, and the Son of Man is being betrayed into the hands of sinners. Mat 26:46 Rise, let us be going. See, My betrayer is at hand." Mat 26:47

10:PM   And while He was still speaking, behold, Judas, one of the twelve, with a great multitude with swords and clubs, came from the chief priests and elders of the people. Mat 26:48 Now His betrayer had given them a sign, saying, "Whomever I kiss, He is the One; seize Him." Mat 26:49 Immediately he went up to Jesus and said, "Greetings, Rabbi!" and kissed Him John 18:6 Now when He said to them, **"I am He," they drew back and fell to the ground**. John 18:7 Then He asked them again, "Whom are you seeking?" And they said, "Jesus of Nazareth." John 18:8 Jesus answered, "I have told you that **I am** He. Therefore, if you seek Me, let these go their way,"

11:PM John 18:9 that the saying might be fulfilled which He spoke, "Of those whom You gave Me I have lost none." John 18:10 Then Simon Peter, having a sword, drew it and struck the high priest's servant, and cut off his right ear. The servant's name was Malchus. John 18:11 So Jesus said to Peter, "Put your sword into the sheath. Shall I not drink the cup which My Father has given Me?"

12:PM Jesus betrayal by Judas and Healing of Malchus Ear cut off by Peter 12 Then the soldiers and the commander and the Jewish officials took Jesus into custody and bound him 13 and led him first to Annas; for he was the father-in-law of Caiaphas, who was high priest that year.

Midnight

1:AM   First Hebrew Trial phase Haesmonian Palace on the west side of the Temple before Annas John 18:19-24 Meanwhile the high priest asked Jesus about his disciples and about his teaching. 20 Jesus answered him, "I have spoken openly to the world, I always taught in a synagogue or at the temple, where all the Jews come together, and I spoke nothing in secret. 21 Why do you ask me? Ask those who heard what I said to them. Look, they know what I said." 22 When he had said these things, one of the nearby officials gave Jesus a blow, saying, "Is this the way you answer the high priest?" 23 Jesus answered him, "If I misspoke, testify concerning the wrong; but if I spoke correctly, why do you strike me?" 24 Then Annas sent him bound to Caiaphas the high priest.

Peter standing outside Annas, the High Priests home, at a fire denies he knows Jesus John 18:25

2:AM   Second Hebrew Trial phase before Caiaphas Mark 14:53 And they led Jesus away to the high priest; and with him were assembled all the chief priests, the elders, and the scribes. Mark 14:54 But Peter followed Him at a distance, right into the courtyard of the high priest. And he sat with the servants and warmed himself at the fire. Mark 14:55 Now the chief priests and all the council sought testimony against Jesus to put Him to death, but found none. Mark 14:56 For many bore false witness against Him, but their testimonies did not agree. Mark 14:57 Then some rose up and bore false witness against Him, saying, Mark 14:58 "We heard Him say, 'I will destroy this temple made with hands, and within three days I will build another made without hands.' " Mark 14:59 But not even then did their testimony agree. Mark 14:60 And the high priest stood up in the midst and asked Jesus, saying, "Do You answer nothing? What is it these men testify against You?" Mark 14:61 But He kept silent and answered nothing. Again the high priest asked Him, saying to Him, "Are You the Christ, the Son of the Blessed?" Mark 14:62 Jesus said, **"I am.** And you will see the Son of Man sitting at the right hand of the Power, and coming with the clouds of heaven." Mark 14:63 **Then the high priest tore his clothes** and said, "What further need do we have of witnesses? Mark 14:64 You have heard the blasphemy! What do you think?" And they all condemned Him to be deserving of death. Mark 14:65 Then some began to spit on Him, and to blindfold Him, and to beat Him, and to say to Him, "Prophesy!" And the officers struck Him with the palms of their hands.

3:AM   Many people gave false testimony

4:AM   Matt 26:62 And the high priest stood up and said, "Have you no answer to make? What is it that these men testify against you?" 63 But Jesus remained silent. **And the high priest said to him, "I adjure you by the living God, tell us if you are the Christ, the Son of God."** 64 Jesus said to him, "You have said so. But I tell you, from now on you will see the Son of Man seated at the right hand of Power and coming on the clouds of heaven." 65 **Then the high priest tore his robes** and said, "He has uttered blasphemy. What further witnesses do we need? You have now heard his blasphemy. 66 What is your judgment?" They answered, "He deserves death." 67 Then they spit in his face and struck him. And some slapped him, 68 saying, "Prophesy to us, you Christ! Who is it that struck you?"

(GOD's law against tearing the clothes of the High Priest (Lev 21:10) 'He who is the high priest among his brethren, on whose head the anointing oil was poured and who **is consecrated to wear the garments, shall not uncover his head nor tear his clothes;** (Lev 21:11) nor shall he go near any dead body, nor defile himself for his father or his mother; (Lev 21:12) nor shall he go out of the sanctuary, nor profane the sanctuary of his God; for the consecration of the anointing oil of his God is upon him: **I am the LORD.)**

5:AM Peter standing outside Caiaphas house and denies knowledge of the Lord and the Cock crows.

6:AM Mar 15:1 **Immediately, in the morning,** the chief priests held a consultation with the elders and scribes and the whole council; and they bound Jesus, led Him away, and delivered Him to Pilate.

(the council chamber was on the South side of the Temple) By now it was early morning and they led Jesus to Pilate's **Headquarters but did not enter because they would be defiled and they wanted to eat the Passover** John 18:28 **7:AM The Gospels narrate four trials and an informal questioning of Jesus,** one Jewish informal and one Jewish formal and three Roman trials. The first started with an informal hearing before Annas (the retired High Priest and father in law of the new High Priest Caiaphas) (John 18:12–14, 19–24), while the Sanhedrin members probably were summoned to gather a quorum for the purpose of staging a more formal trial. A meeting of the highest Jewish body (Matt. 26:57–68; Mark 14:53–65) then led to formal charges and the sending of a delegation to Pilate (Matt. 27:1–2; Luke 22:66–71). The Roman trial consisted of an initial interrogation and verdict of innocence by Pilate (Matt. 27:11–14; John 18:28–38a), followed by an appearance before Herod with the same innocent result (Luke 23:6–12) and a final sentencing before Pilate (Matt. 27:15–31; John 18:38b–19:16).

8:AM   First Roman Trial Phase at the Praetorium with Pilate Presiding (I find no fault in HIM)

9:AM   Pilate pronounces Jesus innocent, but scourges him and crowns him with thorns   John 19:14

John's account of Jesus' Roman trial is by far the most detailed in the Gospels. The entire Roman portion of Jesus' trial is a pattern of outdoor and indoor scenes: outside (18:29–32); inside (18:33–38a); outside (18:38b–40); inside (19:1–3); outside (19:4–7); inside (19:8–11); and outside (19:12–15).

10:AM Second Roman Trial phase at the Fortress of Antonio with Herod Presiding Luke 23:7 (I find no fault in HIM)

11:AM Third Roman Trial phase with Pilate Presiding (I find no fault in HIM)

          "Let Him be crucified!"

Mat 27:24 When Pilate saw that he could not prevail at all, but rather that a tumult was rising, he took water and washed his hands before the multitude, saying, "I am innocent of the blood of this just Person. You see to it." Mat 27:25 And all the people answered and said, "His blood be on us and on our children." Mat 27:26 Then he released Barabbas to them; and when he had scourged Jesus, he delivered Him to be crucified. Now as they came out, they found a man of Cyrene, Simon by name. Him they compelled to bear His cross.

Mat 27:33 And when they had come to a place called Golgotha, that is to say, Place of a Skull,

Mat 27:34 they gave Him sour wine mingled with gall to drink. But when He had tasted it, He would not drink. Mat 27:35 Then they crucified Him, and divided His garments, casting lots, that it might be fulfilled which was spoken by the prophet: "THEY DIVIDED MY GARMENTS AMONG THEM, AND FOR MY CLOTHING THEY CAST LOTS." Mat 27:36 Sitting down, they kept watch over Him there. Mat 27:37 And they put up over His head the accusation written against Him: THIS IS JESUS THE KING OF THE JEWS. Mat 27:38 Then two robbers were crucified with Him, one on the right and another on the left. **12:AM** Crucifixion and the Sky is dark as night Mat 27:45 Now from the sixth hour until the ninth hour there was darkness over all the land. Mat 27:46 And about the ninth hour Jesus cried out with a loud voice, saying, "Eli, Eli, lama sabachthani?" that is, "MY GOD, MY GOD, WHY HAVE YOU FORSAKEN ME?" Mat 27:47 Some of those who stood there, when they heard that, said, "This Man is calling for Elijah!" Mat 27:48 immediately one of them ran and took a sponge, filled it with sour wine and put it on a reed, and offered it to Him to drink. Mat 27:49 The rest said, "Let Him alone; let us see if Elijah will come to save Him." Mat 27:50 And Jesus cried out again with a loud voice, and yielded up His spirit. Mat 27:51 Then, behold, the veil of the temple was torn in two from top to bottom; and the earth quaked, and the rocks were split, Mat 27:52 and the graves were opened; and many bodies of the saints who had fallen asleep were raised; John 19:28 After this, Jesus, knowing that all things were now accomplished, that the Scripture might be fulfilled, said, "I thirst!" John 19:29 Now a vessel full of sour wine was sitting there; and they filled a sponge with sour wine, put it on hyssop, and put it to His mouth. John 19:30 So when Jesus had received the sour wine, He said, "It is finished!" And bowing His head, He gave up His spirit.

John 19:31 Therefore, because it was the Preparation Day, that the bodies should not remain on the cross on the Sabbath (for that Sabbath was a high day), the Jews asked Pilate that their legs might be broken, and that they might be taken away.

1:PM   Sky is dark

2:PM   Sky is still dark and

3:PM   Mark 15:42 Jesus Christ commits his Spirit and Says, "It is finished" and at the Temple the last Passover lamb is sacrificed and the High Priest cries out "It is Finished"

Mat 27:50 And Jesus cried out again with a loud voice, and yielded up His spirit. Then, behold, **the veil of the temple was torn in two from top to bottom; and the earth quaked, and the rocks were split, and the graves were opened; and many bodies of the saints who had fallen asleep were raised; and coming out of the graves**

after His resurrection, they went into the holy city and appeared to many. Mat 27:54 So when the centurion and those with him, who were guarding Jesus, saw the earthquake and the things that had happened, they feared greatly, saying, "Truly this was the Son of God!"

Mark 15:42–47 (ESV) 42 And when evening had come, since it was the day of Preparation, that is, the day before the (High) Sabbath, 43 Joseph of Arimathea, a respected member of the council, who was also himself looking for the kingdom of God, took courage and went to Pilate and asked for the body of Jesus. 44 Pilate was surprised to hear that he should have already died. And summoning the centurion, he asked him whether he was already dead. 45 And when he learned from the centurion that he was dead, he granted the corpse to Joseph. John 19:39 And Nicodemus, who at first came to Jesus by night, also came, bringing a mixture of myrrh and aloes, about a hundred pounds. 46 And Joseph bought a linen shroud, and taking him down, wrapped him in the linen shroud and laid him in a tomb that had been cut out of the rock. And he rolled a stone against the entrance of the tomb. 47 Mary Magdalene and Mary the mother of Jesus saw where he was laid. John 19:38 After this, Joseph of Arimathea, being a disciple of Jesus, but secretly, for fear of the Jews, asked Pilate that he might take away the body of Jesus; and Pilate gave him permission. So he came and took the body of Jesus.

4:PM Luke 23:54 That day was the Preparation, and the Sabbath drew near. Luke 23:55 And the women who had come with Him from Galilee followed after, and they observed the tomb and how His body was laid. Luke 23:56 Then they returned and prepared spices and fragrant oils.

And they rested on the Sabbath according to the commandment.

5:PM Passover meal is in progress and it begins to be the High Sabbath of the Feast of Unleavened Bread a day of no work except to prepare food.

End of the fourth day of the week according to Jewish calendar

High Sabbath of
The Feast of Unleavened Bread
Fifth day of the week

<u>The High Sabbath of the Feast of Unleavened Bread</u> starts during the Passover meal at dusk, and begins the 15th day of the month, according to GOD's command in Exodus 12:16

A High Sabbath is a day with no work allowed except to prepare meals.

The Lord's first night and day in the tomb.

6:PM The continuation of the Passover meal and the beginning of 15th day of the month, a High Sabbath, Jesus' first night in the tomb.

7:PM
8:PM
9:PM
10:PM
11:PM
12:PM   Overnight
1:AM
2:AM
3:AM
4:AM
5:AM
6:AM
7:AM
 8:AM   **The High Sabbath of Unleavened Bread**
                   (a day without work)
9:AM

The Passion of the Christ, 119

10:AM
11:AM
12:AM
1:PM
2:PM
3:PM
4:PM
5:PM

The Passion of the Christ, 120

2nd day of Feast
of Unleavened Bread and First Fruits
The day of Preparation for the Weekly Sabbath
The Lord's second night and day in the tomb.
Sixth day of the week

This is a day of work and commerce and holds two important activities, The Priest can ask Pilate to post a guard troop at the Tomb and the women can buy linen and perfumed oils for properly burying The Lord.

6:PM Continuation of the evening meal and the beginning of **the 16th day of the month.**
7:PM
8:PM
9:PM
10:PM
11:PM
12:PM   Overnight
1:AM
2:AM
3:AM
4:AM
5:AM
6:AM
7:AM   Matthew 27:62–66 (ESV) The Guard at the Tomb 62 The next day, that is, after the day of Preparation, the chief priests and the Pharisees gathered before Pilate and said, "Sir, we remember how that impostor said, while he was still alive, 'After three days I will rise.' Therefore order the tomb to be made secure until the third day, lest his

disciples go and steal him away and tell the people, 'He has risen from the dead,' and the last fraud will be worse than the first." Pilate said to them, "You have a guard of soldiers. Go, make it as secure as you can." So they went and made the tomb secure by sealing the stone and setting a guard.

8:AM   Mar 16:1 Now when the Sabbath was past, Mary Magdalene, Mary the mother of James, and Salome bought spices, that they might come and anoint Him

9:AM

10:AM

11:AM

12:AM

1:PM

2:PM

3:PM

4:PM

5:PM

End of 6th day of the Week according to Jewish calendar and the beginning of the Weekly Sabbath

17th day of the Month,
Weekly Sabbath
Jesus Christ Resurrected on the third day

Third day of the Feast of Unleavened Bread and First Fruits, the Weekly Sabbath without work.

It is the third day in the Lord's entombment (3days and 3 nights and raised on the third day) This will be the day of the resurrection and will mirror the harvesting of the First Fruits of the Barley.

Sabbath

6:PM   The evening meal continues and **the 17th day of the month begins** Luke 23:56 Then they returned and prepared spices and fragrant oils. **And they rested on the Sabbath according to the commandment.**

7:PM

8:PM

9:PM

10:PM

11:PM

12:PM   Overnight

1:AM

2:AM

3:AM

4:AM

5:AM

6:AM

         Weekly Sabbath with no work allowed

7:AM

8:AM
9:AM
10:AM
11:AM
12:AM
1:PM
2:PM
3:PM
4:PM   Mat 27:51…the earth quaked, and the rocks were split, Mat 27:52 and the graves were opened; and many bodies of the saints who had fallen asleep were raised; Mat 27:53   **and coming out of the graves "after His resurrection", they went into the holy city and appeared to many.**

As Jesus arose, they (the Holy ones) arose Matt 27:53, the resurrected saints came out of the graves and were seen in town by the inhabitants and the Priests harvesting the barley for their first Fruits offering were on the same Mount of Olives, where the cemetery was located.

5:PM   **At the end of this day,** the Lord Jesus Christ is resurrected; The Lord of the Sabbath is raised on the Sabbath, three days and three nights after the crucifixion, as the Lord said. At the end of the Sabbath, at the same time, the High Priest goes over to the Mount of Olives to harvest the First Fruits of the Barley to prepare for the offering to be presented at the morning prayers on the first day of the week.

End of the Sabbath according to the Jewish Calendar

18th day of the Month,
First day of the week
The day of the First Fruits offering

Fourth day of the Feast of Unleavened Bread and First Fruits offering

Beginning of the Resurrection 40 Day period

As soon as twilight comes and the First day of the week starts there is a flurry of activity to process the First Fruits of the Barley and the Holy Ones who were resurrected when Jesus was resurrected go into town and are seen by people who knew them. As overnight turns to dawn, the women bringing burial wrappings and perfumed oils find the tomb empty. Mary speaks to Jesus but can't touch Him because he has not ascended to the Father, but later he comes back and visits the disciples.

6:PM   The evening meal continues and **the 18th day of the month begins.**

The Chief Priests are busy preparing the First Fruits offering which was harvested at the end of the Sabbath.

   Mat 27:53 (The Holy ones) and **coming out of the graves "after His resurrection", they went into the holy city and appeared to many.**

7:PM   The Tomb is empty
8:PM   The Tomb is empty
9:PM   The Tomb is empty
10:PM The Tomb is empty
11:PM The Tomb is empty
12:PM The Tomb is empty   Overnight
1:AM   The Tomb is empty

2:AM The Tomb is empty

3:AM The Tomb is empty

4:AM The Tomb is empty

5:AM The Tomb is empty

6:AM Luke 24:1 Now on the first day of the week, very early in the morning, they, and certain other women with them, came to the tomb bringing the spices which they had prepared. Luke 24:2 But they found the stone rolled away from the tomb. Luke 24:3 Then they went in and did not find the body of the Lord Jesus. Luke 24:4 And it happened, as they were greatly perplexed about this, that behold, two men stood by them in shining garments. Luke 24:5 Then, as they were afraid and bowed their faces to the earth, they said to them, "Why do you seek the living among the dead?

Luke 24:6 He is not here, but is risen! Remember how He spoke to you when He was still in Galilee, Luke 24:7 saying, 'The Son of Man must be delivered into the hands of sinful men, and be crucified, and the third day rise again.' " Luke 24:8 And they remembered His words.

Mat 28:1 Now after the Sabbath, as the first day of the week began to dawn, Mary Magdalene and the other Mary came to see the tomb. Mat 28:2 And behold, there was a great earthquake; for an angel of the Lord descended from heaven, and came and rolled back the stone from the door, and sat on it. Mat 28:3 His countenance was like lightning, and his clothing as white as snow. Mat 28:4 And the guards shook for fear of him, and became like dead men. Mat 28:5 But the angel answered and said to the women, "Do not be afraid, for I know that you seek Jesus who was crucified. Mat 28:6 He is not here; for He is risen, as He said. Come, see the place where the Lord lay.

John 20:12 And seeth two angels in white sitting, the one at the head, and the other at the feet, where the body of Jesus had lain. John 20:13 And they say unto her, Woman, why weepest thou? She saith unto them, Because they have taken away my Lord, and I know not where they have laid him. John 20:14 And when she had thus said, she turned herself back, and saw Jesus standing, and knew not that it was Jesus. John 20:15 Jesus saith unto her, Woman, why weepest thou? whom seekest thou? She, **supposing him to be the gardener,** saith unto him, Sir, if thou have borne him hence, tell me where thou hast laid him, and I will take him away. Joh 20:16 Jesus saith unto her, Mary. She turned herself, and saith unto him, Rabboni; which is to say, Master. Joh 20:17 Jesus saith unto her, **Touch me not; for I am not yet ascended to my Father:** but go to my brethren, and say unto them, I ascend unto my Father, and your Father; and to my God, and your God. __But it was not until He had risen from the dead, He who was "the firstborn from the dead"__ (Colossians 1:18), delivered to His Father the "firstfruits of them that slept" (1 Corinthians 15:20), that His disciples, and indeed all who would "believe on |Him| through their word" (John 17:20), could be made "sons of God" (Romans 8:14). "And if children, then heirs; heirs of God, and jointheirs with Christ" (Romans 8:17). This high standing comes as a fulfillment of His determination to "be the firstborn among many brethren" (v. 29).

7:AM Mat 28:11 Now while they were going, behold, some of the guard came into the city and reported to the chief priests all the things that had happened. Mat 28:12

When they had assembled with the elders and consulted together, **the chief priests gave a large sum of money to the soldiers, Mat 28:13 saying, "Tell them, 'His disciples came at night and stole Him away while we slept.' Mat 28:14** And if this comes to the governor's ears, we (Priests and Sanhedrin) will appease him and make you secure." Mat 28:15 So they (the guards) took the money and did as they were instructed; and this saying is commonly reported among the Jews until this day.

8:AM   Jesus Christ ascends to The Father with the Holy ones resurrected with him as his First Fruits

9:AM   First Fruits offering of Barley harvest by the High Priest of the Jews

10:AM Two disciples on the road to Emmaus (Approximately 7 miles from Jerusalem) Luke 24:14 And they talked together of all these things which had happened. Luke 24:15 So it was, while they conversed and reasoned, that Jesus Himself drew near and went with them. Luke 24:16 But their eyes were restrained, so that they did not know Him. Luke 24:17 And He said to them, "What kind of conversation is this that you have with one another as you walk and are sad?" Luke 24:18 Then the one whose name was Cleopas answered and said to Him, "Are You the only stranger in Jerusalem, and have You not known the things which happened there in these days?" Luke 24:19

11:AM And He said to them, "What things?" So they said to Him, "The things concerning Jesus of Nazareth, who was a Prophet mighty in deed and word before God and all the people, Luke 24:20 and how the chief priests and our rulers delivered Him to be condemned to death, and crucified Him. Luke 24:21 But we were hoping that it was He who was going to redeem Israel. Indeed, besides all this, today is the third day since these things happened. Luke 24:22 Yes, and certain women of our company, who arrived at the tomb early, astonished us. Luke 24:23 When they did not find His body, they came saying that they had also seen a vision of angels who said He was alive.

12:AM Luke 24:24 And certain of those who were with us went to the tomb and found it just as the women had said; but Him they did not see." Luke 24:25 Then He said to them, "O foolish ones, and slow of heart to believe in all that the prophets have spoken! Luke 24:26 **Ought not the Christ to have suffered these things and to enter into His glory?" Luke 24:27 And beginning at Moses and all the Prophets, He expounded to them in all the Scriptures the things concerning Himself.** Luke 24:28 Then they drew near to the village where they were going, and He indicated that He would have gone farther.

1:PM Luke 24:29 But they constrained Him, saying, "Abide with us, for it is toward evening, and the day is far spent." And He went in to stay with them. Luke 24:30 Now it came to pass, as He sat at the table with them, that He took bread, blessed and broke it, and gave it to them. Luke 24:31 Then their eyes were opened and they knew Him; and He vanished from their sight. Luke 24:32 And they said to one another, "Did not our heart burn within us while He talked with us on the road, and while He opened the Scriptures to us?" Luke 24:33 So they rose up that very hour and returned to Jerusalem, and found the eleven and those who were with them gathered together, Luke 24:34 saying, "The Lord is risen indeed, and has appeared to

Simon!"
2:PM   Running back to Jerusalem
3:PM   Running back to Jerusalem
4:PM   Returning to Jerusalem
5:PM   Luke 24:35 And they told about the things that had happened on the road, and how He was known to them in the breaking of bread. Luke 24:36 Now as they said these things, **Jesus Himself stood in the midst of them,** and said to them, "Peace to you." Luke 24:37 But they were terrified and frightened, and supposed they had seen a spirit. Luke 24:38 And He said to them, "Why are you troubled? And why do doubts arise in your hearts? Luke 24:39 Behold My hands and My feet, that it is I Myself. Handle Me and see, for a spirit does not have flesh and bones as you see I have."

Luke 24:40 When He had said this, He showed them His hands and His feet. Luke 24:41 But while they still did not believe for joy, and marveled, He said to them, "Have you any food here?" Luke 24:42 So they gave Him a piece of a broiled fish and some honeycomb. Luke 24:43 And He took it and ate in their presence. Luke 24:44 Then He said to them, "These are the words which I spoke to you while I was still with you, that all things must be fulfilled which were written in the Law of Moses and the Prophets and the Psalms concerning Me." Luke 24:45 And He opened their understanding, that they might comprehend the Scriptures. Luke 24:46 Then He said to them, "Thus it is written, and thus it was necessary for the Christ to suffer and to rise from the dead the third day, Luke 24:47 and that repentance and remission of sins should be preached in His name to all nations, beginning at Jerusalem. Luke 24:48

And you are witnesses of these things. Luke 24:49 Behold, I send the Promise of My Father upon you; but tarry in the city of Jerusalem until you are endued with power from on high."

End of the day when the First Fruits offering will be offered.

19th day of the Month, 2nd day of the week
Fifth day of the Feast of Unleavened Bread
Second day of the Resurrection period

444   3rd day   Nisan   20

20th day of the Month, Third day of the week
Sixth day of the Feast of Unleavened Bread
Third day of the Resurrection period

445   4th day   Nisan   21

21st day of the Month, High Sabbath
Seventh Day of the Feast of Unleavened Bread
Fourth day of the Resurrection period.

Conclusion: "The Sacred schedule" of the Passion period of Jesus Christ, is based on GOD's schedule for "His" Feasts. The Lord, Jesus Christ, observed the commandments of GOD. It is important for us to know the truth and understand the Feasts of GOD. This study was not written to change our Holidays but to expose the beauty of the fulfillment of Biblical prophesies and The Unbreakable Promises of our GOD.

Chapter Six

What biblical evidence will tell us the Birth date of our Lord, The Messiah, Jesus Christ?

It is easy to be confused about the chronology of the events surrounding Jesus Christ's birth. Why is it important to know when Jesus was born? In the grand plan of Salvation through the death, burial, and resurrection of Jesus Christ, the information is only of secondary import. But, as a faith building confirmation of GOD honoring his promises to Abraham, Isaac, Jacob, David, and confirming GOD's words through his prophets, it is important. Ecclesiastes 3:15 Reminds us, **"That which is has already been, And what is to be, has already been; And God requires an account of what is past."**

The Bible offers incredible layering of GOD's choreography of events and meaning. Let us not forget the shadow pictures of the birthplace of our Savior Bethlehem-Ephrata. Bethlehem, meaning House of Bread and Ephrata, meaning harvest of the grapes. It is important for us to contemplate that our **Messiah's birthplace is the meeting of the "Bread of Life" and the "Blood of the Covenant".** (Micah 5.2) Bethlehem had large sheepfolds and the High Priest would choose the Passover lamb from Bethlehem and Jesus our Passover lamb was born in Bethlehem. Knowledge of dates, prophecies, and shadow pictures are important and will open up a greater understanding of our GOD.

The most important clue to determining the Birth date of The Messiah, Jesus Christ, is to determine the birth date of John, the Baptist, because our Messiah, is born six months after John, the Baptist. Luke's narrative starts with the introduction of John, the Baptists, parents; **Two important, but small details will provide the structure to date the birth of John, the Baptist and Jesus Christ;** (1). Luke tells us, that **Zechariah is in an order of priestly service named Aviyah.** This information will help us deduce the exact date of the visit from the Angel Gabriel, and then

(2). Gabriel tells Mary that as a sign to her **Elizabeth is 6 months pregnant when Mary becomes pregnant by the Holy Spirit.** The knowledge around these two visitations of Gabriel, give us an almost exact date of the birth of John and then Jesus six months later. And the shadow pictures in the Feasts of GOD will confirm the dates.

Zechariah (whose name means the Lord remembers) married to Elizabeth (whose name means the Oath of GOD) are given a baby boy to answer their prayers, John the Baptist (Grace of Jehovah).

Gabriel speaking to Zechariah Luke 1:14 He will be a joy and a delight to you, and many people will rejoice when he is born, for he will be great in the sight of The Lord (Adonai). He is never to drink wine or other liquor, and he will be **filled with the Holy Spirit even from his mother's womb.** He will turn many of the people of Israel to the Lord, their God. He will go out ahead of Jesus Christ in **the spirit and power of Elijah** to turn the hearts of fathers to their children and the disobedient to the wisdom of the righteous, to make ready for The Lord (Adonai) a people prepared."

John, the Baptist, is born on the day of Passover and is the fulfillment of the empty seat left for the Prophet, Elijah, at the Passover meal.

Jesus Christ (GOD's Salvation) is born on the first day of the Feast of Tabernacles and the scripture says Jesus "Tabernacled" among us John 1:14. The calendar calculations indicate both births to be delivered on a Feast Day six months apart. GOD's Choreography of having the births be a fulfillment of the shadow pictures of GOD's Feast of Passover (Pesach) and Tabernacles (Sukkots) is another confirmation that "what has happened" in the Old Testament is replayed in the New Testament.

Two additional events will exemplify the layering of shadow events in the Bible:
1. Israel left slavery in Egypt 430 years to the day on Passover on their trip to the Promised Land. Exodus 12:41 and **John, the Baptist, born on Passover.**
2. The last recording of time in the Old Testament is in Nehemiah 13:12 At a Feast, the offerings being offered were required at the Feast of Tabernacles. **430 Years to the day in 3/2 BC Jesus Christ was born** to lead us into the promised life during The Feast of Tabernacles. Also Nehemiah 13:30-31confirms telling us this is a First Fruits offering.

Let us follow the clues given in the Gospel of Luke that date the birth of John, the Baptist, and Jesus Christ.

Zechariah, **by secret ballot is chosen** to burn incense to the Lord in the Holy Place. Zechariah, was a member of the priesthood (section / division) of Aviyah. (Luke 1:5). **While serving in the Temple,** Gabriel, the angel, who stands in the presence of Almighty GOD, speaks to Zechariah and tells him that GOD will give him a son and to name him, John. **To date this experience we need to know about the scheduling of the priests.**

The Priests are divided into divisions. There were 24 divisions and there work schedule was based on one division being responsible for the Temple Services each week except during Feast weeks when all divisions worked. 1 Chronicles 24:10 Sets out the Divisions of the Priesthood and their service starting with the first week of the year.

Detail of the Priesthood Divisions work schedule from the beginning of each year: The new year starts on the sighting of the renewed moon in the month that the Barley crop is going to become ripe, called the month of the Aviv.

1st Week   Yahoiariv   division   starting after the Sabbath after the new moon.

Passover,
Unleavened Bread   All Priesthood Divisions Serve
and First Fruits

2nd Week	Yedaiyah division
3rd Week	Harim division
4th Week	Seorim division
5th Week	Malchiyah division
6th Week	Miyamin division
7th Week	Hakkoz division
Pentecost	**All Divisions Serve**
8th Week	Aviyah division (This is the division that

includes Zechariah)

Calculating the timing of Zechariah's meeting with the Angel, Gabriel. (Sivan 9-10, 4BC) The week after Pentecost.

Another clue to help us determine the exact day.
The scriptural reference to the meeting of Zechariah and the Angel, Gabriel, indicates there was a "great multitude" praying while Zechariah entered the Holy Place to burn the incense, this day must be the first day of the week because it is the only day of this week that there will be a great multitude of people at the Temple because this is the High day ending The Feast of Pentecost and the pilgrims will leave Jerusalem tomorrow.

Calculations for the Birth date of John the Baptist.
Therefore, Starting the timing for the conception of John, the Baptist, from the week after Pentecost; Aviyah division of Priesthood finishes service on the 16th day of Sivan and Zechariah starts travel to his home Luke 1:24 "and after these days Elizabeth conceives", 5th day of Tammuz 280 days (9 lunar months 10 days). This date is chosen because

it lines up with

> 1. Gabriel's visit to Zechariah during his Priestly service and
>
> 2. Gabriel's visit to   Mary confirming that Elizabeth is a sign to Mary and is 6 months pregnant.

And isn't it appropriate that Jesus, the "light of the world", would be conceived during the Festival of Lights (Hanukkah) as another layer of GOD's choreography.

Elizabeth' pregnancy and the birth of John the Baptist

Hebrew Months based on the lunar cycle 29.53 days per month

Tammuz	5th day (1)	Partial month
Av		(2) month of pregnancy
Elul		(3) month of pregnancy
Tishri,		(4) month of pregnancy
Heshwan		(5) month of pregnancy
Kislev		(6) month of pregnancy
Shevat		(7) month of pregnancy
Teveth		(8) month of pregnancy
Adar		(9) month of pregnancy

Partial month Aviv (9) 14th Day
Birth of John the Baptist on Passover

By tracking the date clues, we can get the date close, but GOD with the shadow pictures built into His Feasts allows us to confirm his marvelous timing. Isn't it supernatural that John, the Baptist, would be born on Passover, the day that we leave an empty place at the Passover Meal for "The

Prophet" Elijah? And Gabriel's announcement to Zechariah was that John, the Baptist, Ministry would be like that of Elijah.

Birth date of Jesus Christ

Mary's conception in the month of Teveth during Feast of Lights (Hanukkah)

Luke 1:28 **Gabriel visits Mary and tells her she is highly favored!** The Lord is with you…. Vs. 29…You will be with child and give birth to a son and you are to give him the name Jesus…. Vs. 38 I am the Lord's servant, Mary answered, "May it be with me as you have said." Conception approximately the 2nd day of Teveth. **Gabriel gives Mary a sign Luke 1:36 Even Elizabeth, your relative, is going to have a child in her old age, and she who was called barren is in her sixth month. For nothing is impossible with GOD.** Think of the barren women listed in the Bible who prayed to GOD and were blessed with child, Abraham's wife Sarah bore Isaac, Isaac's wife Rebecca bore Jacob, Jacob's wife Leah bore Joseph, Manoah's wife bore Samson, Elkanah's wife Hannah bore Samuel, and Zechariah's wife Elizabeth bore John, the Baptist. And GOD's greatest birth miracle The Virgin Birth of Mary.

Birth of Jesus
Hebrew Months based on the lunar cycle 29.53 days per month
Teveth (partial) month Mary's Conception at the end of the

Feast of Lights (Hanukkah)

Shevat	(2) month of pregnancy
Adar	(3) month of pregnancy
Nisan	(4) 14th Day
	Birth of John the Baptist
	on Passover
Iyyar	(5) month of pregnancy
Sivan	(6) month of pregnancy
Tammuz	(7) month of pregnancy
Av	(8) month of pregnancy
Elul	(9) month of pregnancy
Tishri	(partial) month 15th day

Jesus Christ is born on the First day of the Feast of Tabernacles.
Birth of Jesus (High Sabbath of the Feast of Tabernacles) Tishri 15, 3/2 BC

Six months after the birth of John the Baptist, Jesus Christ, The Messiah, is born on the first day of the Feast of Tabernacles. Eight days later on the Last Great Day of the Feast of Tabernacles, Jesus was circumcised. You may ask why I am sure of these dates, the reason is that there is no other timing that would work with all the other variables and have Jesus at the Temple for his circumcision and the giving of his name. This timing would only align with the timing of the Feast of Tabernacles (Sukkots) and Jesus being in the vicinity to be dedicated at the Jerusalem Temple, after circumcision, instead of a local Synagogue.

Therefore combining scripture with GOD's feast schedule

gives us a clear picture of the timing and choreography of GOD's provision for our salvation. (John 1:14) and the word became flesh and tabernacled among us (Sukkoted or pitched his tent). The choice of words and the shadow pictures that are built in the Bible show us how much our GOD cares for us. GOD's Feast of Tabernacles (Sukkots in Hebrew) is the festival where the pilgrims are to live outside under a covering to remember how GOD provided for Israel the forty years on the way to the Promised Land.

**Additional details
that support the
dating Jesus birth and early childhood:**

1. Scripture tells us that the shepherds were abiding in the fields with their flocks. The shepherds would not be abiding in the field at night in the winter. They are in the sheepfolds at night in the winter, but they would be in the fields at the Feast of Tabernacles.

2. My opinion, GOD did not have HIS Son born outside in the winter. Jerusalem winters are very cold. The temperatures at the Feast of Tabernacles are pleasant.

3. The inns are always full for miles around Jerusalem during GOD's Feasts. At the Barley harvest (Passover), the Wheat harvest (Pentecost), and the grape harvest (Tabernacles).

4. After the birth of Jesus, at the end of Mary's purification period (40 days) Mary and Joseph made the offering for a son at the Temple in Jerusalem, but they offered the sacrifice of two pigeons which is the offering of the poor, so the Magi had not been there to worship and give the Gold, Frankincense, and Myrrh.

5. Mary and Joseph were still in the vicinity of Jerusalem Temple for the prophecies of Anna and Simeon at the Temple, which must be after forty day purification period for Mary, for she would not be allowed to worship at the Temple until then.

6. Scripture tells us two differences in the timing of the visit of the Shepherds and the Wise men. How many months are there from "a baby wrapped in swaddling clothes" to a "small child living in a house" when the Magi

arrived? Herod inquired from the wise men as to when they had seen the star, from that information, Herod put out an order to kill all the male babies in Bethlehem two years and under. Therefore Jesus could have been two years old when the wise men worshipped Jesus with Gold, Frankincense and Myrrh, in Herod's opinion.

7. When did Jesus and family go to Egypt and from where did they depart?

The Birth of Jesus was met with star alignments and with fulfillment of prophesies about stars at his arrival.

The Shepherds did not see stars.
The heavens were alive with signs of the Lord's birth, but the Shepherds were not given a Star to follow, they were given directions. The announcement to the shepherds was by an Angel and a Heavenly Host and they were told where to go in Bethlehem, they did not follow a star. The shepherds saw the baby Jesus in the manger just after his birth.

A King is Coming announced in the stars.
The apparent effect of Jupiter circling over Regulus brings up an important astrological observation. The zero line for beginning and ending the 360 degrees of the Zodiac exists between Cancer and Leo. This means that this motion effect shown by Jupiter circling around Regulus (like a "crown" over the star) was happening in the heavens just east of the zero degree line for astrological measurements. It occurred at the beginning section of the astrological

Zodiac in the view of a culture that studied the stars for direction, calendar, and prophecy and in the case of Gentiles, as part of their religion. This zero line is similar to that adopted by Moses in his arrangement of the armies of Israel in the fashion of the Zodiac around the Tabernacle in the wilderness. The biblical Zodiac designed by Moses also began with the royal sign of Leo, but its zero degree line was located in the middle of the constellation, not at its beginning. **In all cultures, these alignments would surely have shown to the people, of that era, that a great king or ruler was then being introduced to the world.**

The Roman Stargazers had coincidental confirmation of their King and Country.

And who was the greatest ruler then in existence? It was Augustus Caesar, emperor of Rome. Note the chronological significance, the star movement coincided with the 25th year of Augustus' elevation to supreme power over the Romans and the 750th anniversary of the founding of Roman empire. The same exact year the people and Senate of Rome gave Augustus his supreme title: Pater Patriae (the Father of the Country). To those in Rome, it seemed like heaven itself was giving approval for the emperorship of Augustus and that the government of Rome had the divine right to rule the world. Rome, itself, would not have disputed that interpretation and most people would have agreed that the astronomical evidence in support of it was overwhelming.

The Eastern Magi or Chaldeans who had studied in the school of Daniel had another view and understanding.

The Magi (Wise Men or Astrologers) from the eastern world were also watching these wonderful celestial phenomena denoting the advent of "royalty." These Magi did not go to Rome and its festivities and celebrations. Instead, they followed a star in the direction of Jerusalem and Judaea looking for this special child whom they considered to be a very important newborn "King of the Jews."

What does scripture tell us about the signs that the Magi saw and what do we know, with our limited knowledge that the star alignment might explain? Or is the star information we are talking about, a miracle of GOD, and not just a part of a star sequence that the Lord used for his own pleasure.

The Star sequence for the Chaldeans (Magi, wise men) who came from afar.

The announcement of The Messiah's birth, to the Magi, was a star sequence the Magi had been waiting for their entire lives. The Prophet Daniel knew the timing of the appearance of the Messiah, the Redeemer, and was in charge of teaching the Chaldeans (Magi, Wise men) Daniel 2:46-49 and 14:9 who studied the stars in the East. Virtually the entire Mediterranean world looked upon the Star Sequence as announcement of a new Caesar but the Eastern magi trained by Daniel were looking for the New "King of the Jews".

We don't have scripture for the motivation and or the

accumulation of the treasure, the wise men brought, but we know that Daniel was rich and powerful and a eunuch, who had no heirs. It is possible, he set up his wealth to be delivered to the young child, Jesus, for GOD's provision for the trip to Egypt. **One of the compelling reasons** for believing that Daniel was involved is the oddity of the gifts. If you were coming to worship the King of the Jews, would gold, silver, and precious gems be better than gold, incense, and burial balm. It makes sense if Daniel or GOD is selecting the gifts and they are representative of Gold for His divinity, Frankincense for his Priesthood, and Myrrh for his burial.

A second compelling reason to believe that Daniel was involved with the school teaching the Magi is that formation of any star sequence cannot impart knowledge for the Magi to ask King Herod where the King of the Jews is located so they can go and worship Him? Gabriel told Daniel and therefore he could set up the Legacy of the Magi looking for the Star Sequence that heralded the new coming King of the Jews.

Daniel's involvement has another corroborating fact; the Chaldeans (Magi) when they reached Jerusalem were not being led by a star and therefore ask King Herod where the Christ (King of the Jews) was living because they had seen his star.

Important points to remember;
a. There Magi group probably exceeded 100 people.
b. The Star was not leading them at the time they reached

Jerusalem.
c. The prophecy of the Messiah being born in Bethlehem was not written for many years after the death of Daniel. Bethlehem was not a town in Daniel's time.
d. Ephrata was the name of the town before it became known as Bethlehem.
e. Herod asked the scribes and Pharisees where would the "King of the Jews" be born and they told Herod that Micah 5:2 declared that the Messiah would be born in Bethlehem.
f. When the Magi left Herod's Palace "HIS Star" reappeared and was visible in the daytime and the Magi were overjoyed. They followed the star to the house where Jesus lived.

A natural major star connection happened on the day Jesus is born
An hour and twenty minutes before Sunrise on the High Sabbath of GOD's feast of Tabernacles, Tishri 15, 3BC or August 12, 3BC on the Gregorian calendar; the planet Jupiter (the King) rose in conjunction with The Star, Tsedek (The Righteous) and in line with Venus, (The Virgin) the morning star. This planetary alignment would have created a blazing light in the sky. (Mat 2:1)

Now after Jesus was born in Bethlehem of Judea in the days of Herod, the Great, behold, wise men from the East, came to Jerusalem (a minimum of 40 days after the birth) , (Mat 2:2) saying, "Where is He who has been born King of the Jews?" The scribes and Pharisees told them the child was born in Bethlehem. Mat 2:9 When they heard the king, they departed; and behold, the star which they "had seen" in the East went before them, till it came and stood over where **the young Child was.** Mat 2:11 And when they **had come into the house, they saw "the young Child" with Mary, His mother,** and fell down and worshiped Him. And when they had opened their treasures, they presented gifts to Him: gold, frankincense, and myrrh.

The Wise men from the East were as much as 700 miles away in Babylon (Persia) because the Bible says that "when they reached the house of the small child." Jesus was no longer a newborn and he was no longer in a manger but in a house. (Bethlehem or possibly Nazareth.) After the Magi treasures had been given to Jesus, Luke's gospel indicates the Angel appeared and told Joseph and Mary flee to Egypt. Mary and Joseph left immediately for Egypt and returned after Herod's death and upon return from Egypt they settled in Nazareth.

Examining HIS star and the prophesies about His Star
We do have scriptural confirmations of "HIS" star spoken of by the Bible. The only major star sequence we can verify with our astrological knowledge that fits with the timing, also fits with the scriptural star descriptions by Jacob in Genesis 49:10, Numbers 24:17, John in Revelation 12:1, in Matthew 2:1-11, in II Peter 1:16-19 .

The phenomenon is the alignment of Jupiter (the King planet which is located between the legs of the star grouping, Ariel the lion of the Tribe of Judah) and the star Tsedek, the Righteous.

Just below Ariel the lion is Virgo star grouping (Bethula) Venus (the Virgin). Below the two stars "the King" and "the Righteous" was "the Virgin" with the moon and the sun beneath her feet. Rev 12:1

Prophecies of the Messiah and a Star

Blessing on Judah from Jacob
The lion of the Tribe of Judah star grouping, Has a star between the feet of the lion called Melekh (King in Hebrew) or Regulus (King in Latin) or Jupiter (King in Greek).
Gen 49:9 Judah is a lion's whelp; From the prey, my son, you have gone up. He bows down, he lies down as a lion; And as a lion, who shall rouse him?
Gen 49:10 The scepter shall not depart from Judah, Nor a lawgiver from between his feet, Until Shiloh (The Messiah) comes; And to Him shall be the obedience of the people.

Prophesy from Balaam on Israel
Num 24:16 The utterance of him who hears the words of God, And has the knowledge of the Most High, Who sees the vision of the Almighty, Who falls down, with eyes wide open: "I see Him, but not now; I behold Him, but not near; **A Star shall come out of Jacob; A Scepter shall rise out of Israel, And batter the brow of Moab, And destroy all the sons of tumult.**

Heb 1:5-8 For to which of the angels did He ever say: "YOU ARE MY SON, TODAY I HAVE BEGOTTEN YOU"? And again: "I WILL BE TO HIM A FATHER,

AND HE SHALL BE TO ME A SON"? But when He again brings the firstborn into the world, He says: "LET ALL THE ANGELS OF GOD WORSHIP HIM." And of the angels He says: "WHO MAKES HIS ANGELS SPIRITS AND HIS MINISTERS A FLAME OF FIRE."
But to the Son He says: "YOUR THRONE, O GOD, IS FOREVER AND EVER; A SCEPTER OF RIGHTEOUSNESS IS THE SCEPTER OF YOUR KINGDOM.

The star grouping known as Virgo (The Virgin) Venus the Morning Star.
Rev 12:1-5 **Now a great sign was seen in heaven — a woman clothed with the sun, under her feet the moon, and on her head a crown of twelve stars.** She was pregnant and about to give birth, and she screamed in the agony of labor. She bore a male Child who was to rule all nations with a rod of iron. And her Child was caught up to God and His throne.

Another confirming prophesy using the "Morning Star"
2Pe 1:16 For when we made known to you the power and the coming of our Lord Yeshua, the Messiah, we did not rely on cunningly contrived myths. On the contrary, we saw "His Majesty" with our own eyes.
2Pe 1:17-19 For we were there when he received honor and glory from God the Father; and the voice came to him from the grandeur of the Sh'khinah, saying, **"This is my son, whom I love; I am well pleased with him!" We heard this voice come out of heaven when we were with**

him on the holy mountain. Yes, we have the prophetic Word made very certain. You will do well to pay attention to it as to a light shining in a dark, murky place, until the Day dawns and **the Morning Star rises in your hearts.**

This study was not done to change Christmas but instead to follow GOD's word and marvel at the complex interaction of inspired words, people, and events historical, astrological, natural, and miraculous.

After calculating the Sacred calendar based on the lunar cycle of 29.53 days per month self-correcting to the solar calendar with a thirteenth month in the year the barley crop is not ripe (aviv).

Conclusion;   The timing of the Births of Jesus Christ and John the Baptist
Lines up with scripture John 2:20, Luke 3:23
Signs in the sky and
Daniel 9 Prophecy and approximately 299 more scriptural prophetic fulfillments
The Roman Event commemorating Caesar Augustus 25th year and new title as "Pater Patria" Father of the Roman Empire.
Fulfillment of shadow pictures in The Feast of GOD and The Temple and its Implements for Worship.
These are infallible proofs of the Bible and the beauty and faithfulness of our GOD.

It was the early evening of June 17, 2 B.C.E. All the cities around Babylon in Mesopotamia were aglow with talk about a spectacular astronomical event being witnessed in the western sky. What had been monitored for several weeks was the planet Venus moving eastward among the stars on what appeared to be a collision course with the planet Jupiter. Now the expected event had happened right in front of their eyes.

This astronomical drama being enacted in the western part of the sky showed the "coming together" of the two brightest planets in the heavens. The separation between them was so small, they appeared not as two stars, but as one brilliant star shining far brighter than any other star or planet. Though the two planets were millions of miles away from one another, to observers in Babylon in the year of 2 B.C.E., they appeared as a single star dominating the western sky in the direction of Palestine.

The use of superlatives is appropriate in describing this conjunction. Such an awesome display was unique in the lifetimes of people studying the stars for direction, for calculating days of the month, for timing crop planting and superstitions. It would have been especially important to those in Babylon where astronomy and astrological interpretations had been studied and analyzed for centuries. It was celestial pageantry at its best. Such closeness of the planets had not happened for centuries and would not occur again for hundreds of years. At this time in history, such an astronomical phenomenon would have made "the talk of the town" not only in Babylon but also in most regions of the world. The sight would have been observed with a great deal of brilliance in all areas of the earth. Truly, this sighting astonished the world from Rome to China.

Events in Roman History

Example of Tragedy from belief in the stars predicting earthly events instead of GOD's word prophetically announcing events and the Heavens confirming GOD's Word.

One event can give us an example of this "man-made god system". Caesar had the Roman Senate in the year 63 B.C.E order all boy babies to be killed who were born in that year because prophetic dreams and astrological signs suggested that a "King of the Romans" was to be born. The Senate ostensibly considered a "King of the Romans" to be anathema to the government of the Republic. So concerned were some of the senators of this astrological interpretation, whose wives were pregnant, that they refused to register births from their wives in hopes that the signs applied to them. We are informed that in that very year (23 September, 63 B.C.E.), the person who later became the first emperor of the Romans (Augustus) was born.

The motivation of Kings is survival and the motivation of OUR GOD is redemption.

THE END

NOTES

Scripture quoted from
Believer's Bible Commentary
Edited By: Arthur Farstad
By: William MacDonald
Thomas Nelson 1995

"Jesus saith unto her, Touch me not; for I am not yet ascended to my Father: but go to <u>my brethren,</u> and say unto them, I ascend unto <u>my Father, and your Father;</u> and to <u>my God, and your God."</u> (John 20:17)

It is interesting to note that our Lord never called <u>His disciples "brethren"</u> until after His resurrection, and our text, which identifies them as such, was the first thing He uttered after rising from the dead, at least as recorded in Scripture.

Before then, He had referred to them in a variety of ways, including "little children" (John 13:33), "brethren," in the sense of brothers in a family (Matthew 12:49), and even "friends."

<u>"Henceforth I call you not servants;</u> for the servant knoweth not what his lord doeth: but I have called you friends; for all things that I have heard of my Father I have made known unto you" (John 15:15). Certainly the disciples held a special place in Christ's heart.

But it was not until He had risen from the dead, He who

was "the firstborn from the dead" (Colossians 1:18), delivered to His Father the "firstfruits of them that slept" (1 Corinthians 15:20), that His disciples, and indeed all who would "believe on |Him| through their word" (John 17:20), could be made "sons of God" (Romans 8:14). "And if children, then heirs; heirs of God, and jointheirs with Christ" (Romans 8:17). This high standing comes as a fulfillment of His determination to "be the firstborn among many brethren" (v. 29).

He has relabeled the "great congregation" (Psalm 22:22, 25 quoted in Hebrews 2:12) the "church," identifying the individual members as His "brethren," and is not "ashamed" to do so (Hebrews 2:11). As we see in our text, His God is our God, His Father is our Father; in all ways, we who have believed on Him are His brothers. Oh, what a standing is ours!

"And they overcame him by the blood of the Lamb, and by the word of their testimony; and they loved not their lives unto the death." (Revelation 12:11)

This is the last reference in the Bible to the shed blood of the Lord Jesus Christ; here it is the overcoming blood, enabling believers to withstand the deceptions and accusations of Satan.

There are at least 43 references to the blood of Christ in the New Testament, all testifying to its great importance in the salvation and daily life of the believer. Judas the betrayer spoke of it as "innocent blood" (Matthew 27:4), and Peter called it "the precious blood of Christ, as of a lamb without blemish and without spot" (1 Peter 1:19). It is the cleansing blood in 1 John 1:7 and the washing blood in Revelation 1:5, stressing that it removes the guilt of our sins.

Paul calls it the purchasing blood in Acts 20:28 and the redeeming blood twice (Ephesians 1:7; Colossians 1:14; see also 1 Peter 1:18-19; Revelation 5:9), thus declaring the shedding of His blood to be the very price of our salvation. Therefore, it is also the justifying blood (Romans 5:9) and the peacemaking blood (Colossians 1:20). Its efficacy does not end with our salvation, however, for it is also the sanctifying blood (Hebrews 13:12). There is infinite and eternal power in the blood of Christ, for it is "the blood of the everlasting covenant" (v. 20).

The first reference in the New Testament to His blood stresses this aspect. Jesus said at the last supper, "This is my blood of the new testament |same as 'covenant'|, which is shed for many for the remission of sins" (Matthew 26:28). Let no one, therefore, ever count the "blood of the covenant . . . an unholy thing" (Hebrews 10:29), for the blood of Christ is forever innocent, infinitely precious, perfectly justifying, always cleansing, and fully sanctifying.

Jesus Before Caiaphas and the Council
57 Then those who had seized Jesus led him to Caiaphas the high priest, where the scribes and the elders had gathered. 58 And Peter was following him at a distance, as far as the courtyard of the high priest, and going inside he sat with the guards to see the end. 59 Now the chief priests

and the whole council were seeking false testimony against Jesus that they might put him to death, 60 but they found none, though many false witnesses came forward. At last two came forward 61 and said, "This man said, 'I am able to destroy the temple of God, and to rebuild it in three days.' " 62 And the high priest stood up and said, "Have you no answer to make? What is it that these men testify against you?" 63 But Jesus remained silent. And the high priest said to him, "I adjure you by the living God, tell us if you are the Christ, the Son of God." 64 Jesus said to him, "You have said so. But I tell you, from now on you will see the Son of Man seated at the right hand of Power and coming on the clouds of heaven." 65 Then the high priest tore his robes and said, "He has uttered blasphemy. What further witnesses do we need? You have now heard his blasphemy. 66 What is your judgment?" They answered, "He deserves death." 67 Then they spit in his face and struck him. And some slapped him, 68 saying, "Prophesy to us, you Christ! Who is it that struck you?"

Peter Denies Jesus

The Holy Bible: English Standard Version. 2001 (Mt 26:57–69). Wheaton: Standard Bible Society.

2. Jesus Questioned by the High Priest, Denied by Peter (18:12–27)

The Gospels narrate two trials of Jesus, two Jewish and two Roman. The former started with an informal hearing before Annas (18:12–14, 19–24), while Sanhedrin members probably were summoned for the purpose of staging a more formal trial. A meeting of the highest Jewish body (Matt. 26:57–68; Mark 14:53–65) then led to formal charges and the sending of a delegation to Pilate (Matt. 27:1–2; Luke 22:66–71). The Roman trial consisted of an initial interrogation and verdict of innocence by Pilate (Matt. 27:11–14; John 18:28–38a), followed by an appearance before Herod with the same innocent result (Luke 23:6–12) and a final summons before Pilate (Matt. 27:15–31; John 18:38b–19:16).

Though Jewish law contained numerous stipulations regarding legal proceedings against those charged with serious offenses, many such stipulations could be breached if the matter was judged to be urgent (including the possibility of mob violence). Another factor in Jesus' case was that executions could proceed on feast days but not on a Sabbath. Thus, if Jesus' arrest took place on Thursday evening, little time remained if he was to be tried and put to death by the onset of Sabbath at sundown of the following day. Moreover, Roman officials such as Pilate worked only from dawn until late morning, so that the Jews' case against Jesus had to be prepared overnight.4

The present section oscillates between Jesus' informal hearing before Annas (18:12–14, 19–24) and Peter's denials of Jesus (18:15–18, 25–27). By providing an account of Jesus' appearance before Annas, John again fills an important gap, since the Synoptics do not record this event but rather focus exclusively on the formal Jewish trial before Caiaphas. By way of background: Annas was deposed by the Romans in A.D. 15; his son-in-law Caiaphas held the high priesthood from A.D. 18–36 ("the high priest that year" in 18:13 means "the high priest at that time").

a. Jesus taken to Annas (18:12–14)
b. Peter's first denial (18:15–18)
c. Jesus before the high priest (18:19–24)
d. Peter's second and third denials (18:25–27)

Exegesis and Exposition

12Then the soldiers and the commander and the Jewish officials took Jesus into custody and bound him 13and led him first to Annas; for he was the father-in-law of Caiaphas, who was high priest that year. 14(Now Caiaphas was the one who had counseled the Jewish leaders that it would be better for one man to die on behalf of the people.)

15So Simon Peter and another disciple were following Jesus. Now that disciple was known to the high priest and went with Jesus into the high priest's courtyard. 16But Peter stood by the door outside. Then the other disciple, who was known to the high priest, came and talked to the girl at the door and brought Peter in. 17The servant girl at the door said to Peter, "You aren't one of this man's disciples too, are you?" He said, "I'm not." 18Now the servants and officials who stood there had made a fire, because it was cold, and were warming themselves.

19Meanwhile the high priest asked Jesus about his

disciples and about his teaching. 20Jesus answered him, "I have spoken openly to the world, I always taught in a synagogue or at the temple, where all the Jews come together, and I spoke nothing in secret. 21Why do you ask me? Ask those who heard what I said to them. Look, they know what I said." 22When he had said these things, one of the nearby officials gave Jesus a blow, saying, "Is this the way you answer the high priest?" 23Jesus answered him, "If I misspoke, testify concerning the wrong; but if I spoke correctly, why do you strike me?" 24Then Annas sent him bound to Caiaphas the high priest.

25Meanwhile Simon Peter was standing and warming himself. Then they said to him, "You aren't one of his disciples too, are you?" He denied it and said, "I'm not." 26One of the high priest's servants, a relative of the one whose ear Peter had cut off, said, "I saw you in the garden with him, didn't I?" 27So again Peter denied it, and at once a rooster began to crow.

a. Jesus Taken to Annas (18:12–14)

18:12–14   Jesus' preliminary hearing before Annas is recorded only in John. Apparently, in deference to Annas's continuing power and stature, Jesus was first brought to him. The absence of witnesses suggests that this hearing was informal. In the ensuing narrative John alternates between Jesus' hearing before Annas (18:12–14, 19–24) and Peter's denials (18:15–18, 25–27). He uses a similar oscillating pattern in his narration of Jesus' trial before Pilate (see introduction to 18:28–40).

The detachment of soldiers, its commander (by implication), and the Jewish officials, were first introduced in 18:3. To be "bound" (δέω, deō) is a customary expression in conjunction with arrest or imprisonment (e.g., Acts 9:2, 14, 21; earlier in Plato, Leges 9.864E). Yet while powerless in human terms, Jesus' spirit is unbroken (cf. 18:23; see Schnackenburg 1990: 3.233). "First" anticipates the later arraignment before Caiaphas (Ridderbos 1997: 578; Morris 1995: 664; Barrett 1978: 524).

Annas held the office of high priest from A.D. 6 until A.D. 15. He was appointed by Quirinius, the Roman prefect and governor of Syria, and removed from office by Pilate's predecessor, Valerius Gratus (A.D. 15–26) (cf. Josephus, Ant. 18.2.2 §34). Annas continued to wield considerable influence, not only because his removal from office was deemed arbitrary by many Jews, but also because as many as five of his sons, as well as Joseph Caiaphas his son-in-law, held the office at one point or another (Ant. 20.9.1 §§197–98 [A.D. 6–41]).

Thus, even though Caiaphas held the official position of high priest that year (in the sense of "at that time" [Morris 1995: 664]), many still considered Annas, the patriarch of this preeminent high-priestly family, to be the real high priest (Morris 1995: 663; Carson 1991: 581), especially since under Mosaic legislation the appointment was for life (Num. 35:25). Caiaphas, the high priest that year, was the one who had counseled the Jewish leaders that it would be better (more accurate than "good" as in the TNIV) for one man to die on behalf of the people (see commentary at

11:49–52).

Under Roman occupation, the high priests were the dominant political leaders of the Jewish nation (Smallwood 1962). The mention of Caiaphas in 18:14 may serve the purpose of reminding John's readers of Caiaphas's and the Sanhedrin's opinion about Jesus, thus rendering a full account of the hearing held later that night unnecessary (Ridderbos 1997: 578–80; Morris 1995: 671); presumably, John judged that the information regarding this hearing had "been adequately circulated elsewhere" (i.e., in the Synoptic Gospels) (Carson 1991: 581).

b. Peter's First Denial (18:15–18)

18:15–18   At this point in his narrative the evangelist skillfully interposes Peter's initial denial of Jesus; his second and third denials follow in 18:25–27. The "other disciple" known to the high priest is probably none other than "the disciple Jesus loved" (i.e., the apostle John).13 John was a fisherman, but this does not mean that he came from an inferior social background. John's father, Zebedee, is presented in Mark 1:20 as a man having hired servants, and either John and his brother James or their mother (or both) had prestigious ambitions (Matt. 20:20–28 par.). Moreover, it is not impossible that John himself came from a priestly family (Morris 1995: 666 n. 37). "Known" (γνωστός, gnōstos [used in 18:15, 16]) may suggest more than mere acquaintance.

Where was the high priest's courtyard? The official high

priest was Caiaphas, though Annas may have been referred to under this designation as well (see commentary at 18:13). Presumably, he lived in the Hasmonean palace on the west hill of the city, which overlooked the Tyropoeon Valley and faced the temple. It is possible that Caiaphas and Annas lived in the same palace, occupying different wings bound together by a common courtyard. The sequence of references to "the high priest" in this chapter (esp. 18:13–14, 19, 24) shows that Annas is in view and that the courtyard (αὐλή, aulē) is the atrium connected with his house (Carson 1991: 582; contra Barrett 1978: 526).

The mention of a "girl at the door" confirms that the scene took place outside the temple area, for there only men held such assignments (Carson 1991: 582; see further below). Caiaphas's quarters may have shared the same courtyard, so that even the second stage of the investigation would have been relatively private (though with at least some Sanhedrin members present). The formal action taken by the Sanhedrin (at about dawn) is not recorded in John's Gospel (cf. Matt. 27:1–2 pars.). The "other disciple" known to the high priest spoke to "the servant girl on duty" (TNIV; more literally, "the servant girl at the door") and brought Peter in. Apparently, this doorkeeper was a domestic female slave, probably of mature age, since her role was one of responsibility, requiring judgment and life experience.19

The girl's question to Peter, though apparently worded as if expecting a negative answer (Ridderbos 1997: 582; Morris 1995: 667; R. Brown 1970: 824), may more likely be viewed as a cautious assertion (Carson 1991: 583; Barrett 1978: 526, citing J. H. Moulton). "You too" may allude to the "other disciple" (Carson 1991: 583; Barrett 1978: 526; Schlatter 1948: 333; contra R. Brown [1970: 824], who says that the reference is to the disciples with Jesus when he was arrested). Peter's reply is characterized by maximum terseness: "I'm not" (Ridderbos 1997: 582). Perhaps Peter simply wanted to get access to the courtyard without having to engage in conversation with this woman (Carson 1991: 583).

It was cold (cf. 10:22). Nights in Jerusalem, which is half a mile above sea level, can be quite cold in the spring. The servants and officials (referring to "the domestic servants of the high priest" and the "officers of the Sanhedrin" respectively [Ridderbos 1997: 582 n. 42; Morris 1995: 667 n. 42]) had returned to their barracks, entrusting the role of guarding Jesus to the temple guards. Only John mentions that the fire was a charcoal fire (ἀνθρακιά, anthrakia; cf. 21:9; see Carson 1991: 583). The presence of a fire confirms that these preliminary proceedings against Jesus took place at night, when the cold would move people to make a fire to stay warm. Even at night, fires were not normally lit, other than in exceptional circumstances,22 and night proceedings generally were regarded as illegal (Carson 1991: 583). Moreover, the fact that a fire was kept burning in the chamber of immersion so that the priests on night duty could warm themselves there, and that lamps were burning even along the passage that leads below the temple building (m. Tamid 1.1), suggests that the courtyard referred to in the present passage is private.

The description of Peter here suggests that he was trying to be as inconspicuous as possible (Ridderbos 1997: 582). Like Judas earlier (18:5), Peter here "stands" with Jesus' enemies (Michaels 1989: 309; Stibbe 1993: 182).

c. Jesus Before the High Priest (18:19–24)

18:19–21 The conjunction οὖν (oun, meanwhile) indicates that John now resumes his account of Jesus' hearing before Annas (from 18:12–14; see Ridderbos 1997: 582). Again, Annas is referred to as "the high priest" (Carson 1991: 583; contra Barrett 1978: 525). The appropriateness of such a designation even after such an official was removed from office is confirmed by the Mishnah (m. Hor. 3.1–2, 4) and by Josephus (J.W. 2.12.6 §243; cf. 4.3.7–9 §§151–60). There may even be an element of defiance in the Jewish practice of continuing to call previous high priests by that name, challenging the Roman right to depose officials whose tenure was meant to be for life according to Mosaic legislation (cf. Num. 35:25). Apparently, the seasoned, aged Annas still wielded considerable high-priestly power while his relatives held the title.

The fact that Jesus is questioned—a procedure considered improper in formal Jewish trials, where a case had to rest on the weight of witness testimony (e.g., m. Sanh. 6.2)—suggests that the present hearing was more informal. The question addressed to Jesus regarding his disciples and his teaching (διδαχή, didachē [cf. Rev. 2:14–15]) suggests that the authorities' primary concern was theological, despite the political rationale given to Pilate (cf. 19:7, 12).

The Jewish leadership seems to have viewed Jesus as a false prophet (see, later, b. Sanh. 43a) who secretly enticed people to fall away from the God of Israel—an offense punishable by death (Deut. 13:1–11). Apparently, Annas hopes that Jesus might incriminate himself on those counts. Jesus does not directly address the question from the high priest, who already knew the answer in any case (Ridderbos 1997: 582–83), but merely points to the public nature of his instruction. Jesus' (non)answer takes the attention off his disciples and places it squarely upon himself (note the emphatic "I" statements in 18:20–21). The point of Jesus' reference to the public nature of his instruction seems to be that the Jewish authorities would have been more than able to gather eyewitness testimony from those who had heard Jesus teach.29 "Temple" refers to the temple precincts, usually translated "temple courts" in the TNIV (cf. 2:14; 7:14, 28; 8:20; 10:23; see Wallace 1996: 561 n. 15).

"I spoke nothing in secret." Jesus' words here echo those of Yahweh in the Book of Isaiah (e.g., 45:19; 48:16; see R. Brown 1970: 826; Schlatter 1948: 334). The point is not that Jesus never spoke privately with his disciples but that his message was the same in private and in public (Morris 1995: 669; Carson 1991: 584; Borchert 2002: 232); he was not guilty of plotting a sinister conspiracy. Jesus' statement may also seek to establish an ironic contrast between the charge that he pursued his teaching ministry in a secretive fashion (which is manifestly untrue) and the covert way in which the authorities went about Jesus' arrest (enlisting Judas, coming at night, etc.) (see Westcott 1908: 2.276).

"Why ask me? Ask those who heard me. Look, they know what I said." Jesus' challenge is understandable, especially if the questioning of prisoners was considered improper in his day (see commentary at 18:19). This is further confirmed by the recognized legal principle that a person's own testimony regarding himself was deemed invalid (see 5:31). Though an accused person could raise an objection (which must be heard [see 7:50–51]), a case was to be established by way of testimony, whereby witnesses for the defendant were to be questioned first (m. Sanh. 4.1; cf. Matt. 26:59–63 par.). If the testimony of witnesses agreed on essential points, the fate of the accused was sealed. The violation of this formal procedure here strongly suggests that Jesus' hearing before Annas was unofficial (R. Brown 1970: 826).

"Ask those who heard me." Jesus is not being uncooperative and evasive, but rather he urges a proper trial in which evidence is established by interrogation of witnesses; the present informal hearing did not meet such qualifications (Morris 1995: 669). This assertive display of self-confidence before authority was in all likelihood startling. As Josephus shows, those charged would normally maintain an attitude of humility before their judges, assuming "the manner of one who is fearful and seeks mercy" (Ant. 14.9.4 §172; see Schlatter 1948: 335). The official (ὑπηρέτης, hypēretēs) who strikes Jesus in response is one of the temple guards mentioned earlier as having taken part in his arrest (see 18:3, 12).

18:22–24   The official dealt Jesus a blow in the

face—another illegal action. This insult (R. Brown 1970: 826; Moloney 1998: 491) is not the only ill-treatment that Jesus had to endure during his Jewish trial before the Sanhedrin. According to Matthew, "They spit in his face and struck him with their fists. Others slapped him" (26:67). The term used here (ῥάπισμα, rhapisma)denotes a sharp blow with the flat of one's hand (cf. Isa. 50:6 LXX). Striking a prisoner was against Jewish law (Morris 1995: 670; Keener 1993: 307). Compare the similar incident involving Paul in Acts 23:1–5, where the high priest Ananias ordered those standing near Paul to strike him on the mouth.

"Is this the way you answer the high priest?" A proper attitude toward authority was legislated by Exod. 22:28: "Do not blaspheme God or curse the ruler of your people" (quoted by Paul in Acts 23:5; see Ridderbos 1997: 583; R. Brown 1970: 826). "If I said something wrong" (TNIV) reads more literally, "spoke in an evil manner," that is, "if I said something that dishonored the high priest." Jesus implicitly refers to the law of Exod. 22:28 and denies having violated it. The LXX uses the expression "speak evil" for cursing the deaf and blind (Lev. 19:14), one's parents (Lev. 20:9), the king and God (Isa. 8:21), and the sanctuary (1 Macc. 7:42) (Moloney 1998: 488).

Annas's only response is to send Jesus, still bound, to Caiaphas the high priest (Ridderbos 1997: 583). Before Jesus can be brought to Pilate, charges must be confirmed by the official high priest, Caiaphas, in his function as president of the Sanhedrin (Alexander 1988: esp. 46–49;

Schürer 1973–79: 2.199–226). Precisely where the Sanhedrin met at that time is subject to debate; a chamber on the south side of the temple or the marketplace are both cited (Blinzler 1959: 112–14).37 In any case, "sent" need not imply movement to another building but may merely refer to changing courtrooms in the temple.

d. Peter's Second and Third Denials (18:25–27)

18:25–27 Again, John shifts back to Peter (δέ, in the meantime; see R. Brown 1970: 827), who has already denied his Lord once (18:15–18; see Ridderbos 1997: 584). The "they" who spoke to Peter in 18:25 may have been the same (Mark) or a different girl (Matthew) or a group (cf. Luke; see Morris 1995: 672). The connotation of the question in 18:25 closely conforms to that in 18:17. The repetition of "warming himself" in 18:18 and 18:25, rather than being redundant or incongruous, reflects a literary device frequently used in Greek literature to resume the thread of a previous narrative, especially in cases where two plot lines are developed side by side.

The third question heightens Peter's discomfort further in light of who asked it: the man was a relative of Malchus, whose ear Peter had cut off. Being one of Jesus' disciples was not a legal offense, though it could have been surmised that open confession of Jesus might lead to trouble, especially if he was found guilty and executed (cf. 20:19). Of more immediate concern for Peter might have been the earlier incident in which he had drawn a weapon (perhaps carried illegally) and assaulted one of the high priest's servants. Peter's denial of association with Jesus may therefore stem from a basic instinct of self-preservation and a self-serving desire not to incriminate himself in this matter that may have led to legal troubles of his own.42

At once a rooster began to crow (see commentary at 13:38). Mark (14:72) notes that it was then that Peter remembered Jesus' prediction and broke down and wept; John immediately moves on to Jesus' encounter with Pilate. Exactly when cocks crowed in first-century Jerusalem is subject to debate; estimates range from between 12:30 and 2:30 A.M. to between 3:00 and 5:00 A.M. Some have argued that the present reference is not to the actual crowing of a rooster but to the trumpet signal given at the close of the third watch, named "cockcrow" (midnight to 3:00 A.M.) (Bernard 1928: 2.604). If so, then Jesus' interrogation by Annas and Peter's denials would have concluded at around 3:00 A.M.

3. Jesus Before Pilate (18:28–19:16a)

John's account of Jesus' Roman trial is by far the most detailed in the Gospels. The entire Roman portion of Jesus' trial is narrated by John in seven units with an oscillating pattern of outdoor and indoor scenes: outside (18:29–32); inside (18:33–38a); outside (18:38b–40); inside (19:1–3); outside (19:4–7); inside (19:8–11); and outside (19:12–15). This "carefully planned structure" is intended "to exhibit the paradoxical outcome of the whole process—how they [Pilate and the Jewish leaders] found each other in a single unprincipled alliance against Jesus" (Ridderbos 1997: 587;

cf. Acts 4:27).

By now it is early morning. Mark seems to indicate that the chief priests held a second Sanhedrin meeting to lend their actions the appearance of legality (Mark 15:1). After this the Jews lead Jesus from Caiaphas to the palace of the Roman governor. Throughout the following proceedings, Pilate displays the customary reluctance of Roman officials to get involved in internal Jewish religious affairs. Although Pilate keeps referring to Jesus somewhat mockingly as "king of the Jews," the Jews claim to have no king but Caesar. If Pilate were to let Jesus go, he would prove himself to be no friend of Caesar. He sees no choice but to acquiesce to their demands.

a. Jesus interrogated by Pilate (18:28–40)
b. Jesus sentenced to be crucified (19:1–16a)

Exegesis and Exposition

18:28Then they led Jesus from Caiaphas to the Praetorium. By now it was early morning, and in order not to defile themselves they did not enter the Praetorium, so that they would be able to eat the Passover.

29So Pilate came out to them and said, "What charge are you bringing against this man?" 30They answered and said to him, "If he were not a criminal, we would not have handed him over to you." 31Then Pilate said to them, "You take him and judge him according to your own law." The Jews said to him, "It is not lawful for us to execute anyone." 32([This happened] so that the word of Jesus might be fulfilled which he had spoken indicating by what kind of death he was going to die.)

33Then Pilate entered the Praetorium again, and called Jesus and said to him, "Are you the king of the Jews?" 34Jesus answered, "Are you saying this on your own accord or did others talk to you about me?" 35Pilate answered, "Am I a Jew? Your own nation and the chief priests handed you over to me. What have you done?"

36Jesus answered, "My kingdom is not of this world. If my kingdom were of this world, my servants would fight, so that I would not be handed over to the Jews. But now my kingdom is not from here." 37Then Pilate said to him, "Then you are a king, aren't you?" Jesus answered, "You say that I'm a king. I was born for this purpose, and for this purpose I came into the world: to bear witness to the truth. Everyone who is of the truth listens to my voice." 38Pilate said to him, "What is truth?"

And having said this, he went out to the Jews again and said to them, "I find no basis for a charge against him. 39You have a custom that I release for you one prisoner at the Passover. Would you therefore like me to release to you 'the king of the Jews'?" 40Then they cried out again, saying, "Not this one, but Barabbas!" Now Barabbas was a revolutionary.

19:1So, then, Pilate took Jesus and had him flogged. 2And the soldiers twisted together a crown of thorns and placed it on his head and wrapped him in a dark red robe. 3And they kept coming to him and were saying, "Hail, king of the Jews!" And they buffeted him with blows.

4And Pilate came out again and said to them, "Look, I bring him out to you, so that you may know that I find no basis for a charge against him." 5Then Jesus came outside, wearing the thorny crown and the dark red robe. And he [Pilate] said to them, "See, the man!" 6So when the chief priests and the officials saw him, they cried out, saying, "Crucify! Crucify!" Pilate said to them, "You take him and crucify him. I find no basis for a charge against him." 7The Jews answered him, "We have a law, and according to that law he ought to die, because he made himself out to be the Son of God."

8Now when Pilate heard this statement, he grew even more afraid, 9and entered the Praetorium again and said to Jesus, "Where do you come from?" But Jesus gave him no answer. 10Then Pilate said to him, "Will you not talk to me? You realize, don't you, that I have authority to release you and I have authority to crucify you?" 11Jesus answered, "You wouldn't have any authority over me unless it had been given to you from above; for this reason the one who handed me over to you has a greater sin." 12From this moment on Pilate sought to release him; but the Jews cried out, saying, "If you release him, you are no friend of Caesar. Everyone who makes himself out to be a king opposes Caesar."

13So when Pilate heard these words, he led Jesus out and

sat down on the judgment seat at a place called Lithostratos (Gabbatha in Aramaic). 14Now it was the day of preparation of Passover week, about the sixth hour [noon]. And he said to the Jews, "See, your king!" 15Then they cried out, "Take him away, take him away! Crucify him!" Pilate said to them, "Shall I crucify your king?" The chief priests answered, "We have no king but Caesar." 16aSo, then, he gave him over to them, so that he might be crucified.

a. Jesus Interrogated by Pilate (18:28–40)

18:28 Jesus was led to the Praetorium, the headquarters of the Roman governor. Though based in Caesarea in a palace built by Herod the Great (cf. Acts 23:33–35), Pilate, like his predecessors, made it a practice to go up to Jerusalem for high feast days in order to be at hand for any disturbance that might arise. It is unclear whether Pilate's Jerusalem headquarters is to be identified with the Herodian palace on the Western Wall (suggested by the TNIV's "palace") or the Fortress of Antonia (named after Mark Antony [Josephus, J.W. 1.21.1 §40]) northwest of the temple grounds.

Herod the Great had both palaces built, the former in 35 B.C. (on the site of an older castle erected by John Hyrcanus [Josephus, Ant. 18.4.3 §91]), the latter in 23 B.C., whereby especially Philo identifies the (former) Herodian palace as the usual Jerusalem headquarters of Roman governors. Yet the discovery of massive stone slabs in the Fortress of Antonia in 1870 has convinced some that it is this building that is in view (see further commentary at 19:13; see also Vincent 1954). On balance, the Herodian palace is more likely, especially in light of the aforementioned evidence from Philo and Josephus.

"Early morning" is ambiguous. The last two watches of the night (from midnight to 6:00 A.M.) were called "cockcrow" and "early morning" by the Romans. If this is the way the term is used here, then Jesus was brought to Pilate before 6:00 A.M. This coheres with the practice, followed by many Roman officials, of starting the day very early and finishing their workday by late morning. Because Jews rarely tried capital cases at night (see commentary at 18:18), "early morning" more likely means some time after sunrise, when the Sanhedrin had met in formal session and pronounced its verdict on Jesus (Matt. 27:1–2 pars.).9

The references to the Jews not entering the palace in order to avoid ceremonial uncleanness so that they could eat the Passover serves the purpose of explaining Pilate's comings and goings. There is deep irony in the fact that the Jews are scrupulously avoiding ceremonial uncleanness while not being concerned about burdening themselves with the moral guilt of condemning an innocent man to death. Also ironic is that they use a Gentile to achieve their ends yet will not enter a Gentile's house (R. Brown 1970: 866). Jews who entered Gentile homes were considered to contract uncleanness,11 which prevented them from celebrating Passover.

18:30–32 Rather than providing specific charges, the Jews

answer somewhat evasively (Morris 1995: 676), "If he were not a criminal [cf. Matt. 27:23], we would not have handed him over to you." The Jews' response tacitly acknowledges their inability to "bring a water-tight charge against Jesus" (Schnackenburg 1990: 3.245) and reveals their distaste for Roman interference in their own affairs. By calling Jesus a "criminal," they "seek both to impress on Pilate the danger Jesus presents to the public order and at the same time to avoid a concrete charge" (Ridderbos 1997: 590–91).

Pilate, for his part, was well aware of the weakness of the Jews' case against Jesus: "You take him and judge him according to your own law." Like Gallio after him (Acts 18:14–15), Pilate was not interested in being a judge of internal Jewish disputes. The Jews reply, "It is not lawful for us to execute anyone." Despite instances where the Jewish authorities are involved in executions (all of which involved lynch law or breaches of authority) the Sanhedrin did not have the power of capital punishment.21 This was consistent with general Roman practice in provincial administration, and capital punishment was the most jealously guarded of all governmental powers (Sherwin-White 1963: 24–47, esp. 36).

Moreover, an equestrian procurator such as Pilate in an insignificant province such as Judea had no assistants of high rank who could help him carry out his administrative and judicial duties. Thus, he had to rely on local officials in minor matters while retaining the right to intervene in major cases, including "crimes for which the penalty was hard labor in mines, exile, or death." Also, in handling criminal trials, the prefect or procurator was not bound by Roman law that applied only to Roman citizens and cities.23 For this reason, it is difficult to determine with certainty Pilate's motives in offering to give the case back to the Jewish authorities.

Crucifixion was looked upon by the Jews with horror. Execution on a cross was considered to be the same as hanging (Acts 5:30; 10:39), for which Mosaic law enunciated the principle "Anyone who is hung on a tree is under God's curse" (Deut. 21:23; cf. Gal. 3:13). If Jesus had been put to death by the Sanhedrin, stoning would have been the likely mode of execution, since it is the penalty specified in the OT for blasphemy,25 the most common charge against Jesus in John. Other forms of capital punishment sanctioned by mishnaic teaching are burning, beheading, and strangling (m. Sanh. 7.1).

The statement "[This happened] so that the word of Jesus might be fulfilled which he had spoken indicating by what kind of death he was going to die" once again underscores the notions of Jesus' supernatural foresight (cf. 18:4) and of divine sovereignty and theodicy. There are also verbal links with the Johannine "lifted-up" sayings (12:32–33) and the destiny predicted of Peter at his commissioning (21:19). John's point is that even the fact that the Romans had ultimate jurisdiction over capital punishment coheres with Jesus' prediction that he was going to be "lifted up," a Johannine euphemism for crucifixion (Carson 1991: 592).

The Passion of the Christ, 177

18:33–35 After this interchange, Pilate went back inside the palace to interrogate Jesus. In contrast to Jewish practice (see commentary at 18:19, 21), Roman law made provisions for detailed questioning of persons charged with crimes, whether they were Roman citizens (accusatio) or not (cognitio) (Sherwin-White 1963: 13–23). These hearings were public and gave the accused person sufficient opportunity for self-defense against the charges, as seems to be presupposed in Jesus' case by the Synoptics.

The question "Are you the king of the Jews?" is recorded in all four Gospels (Bammel 1984: 417–19). One wonders if Pilate, upon seeing this prisoner bound before him, has a first impression of incredulity: Is this the man accused of claiming to be king of the Jews? (Ridderbos 1997: 593; Morris 1995: 679). If so, then the personal pronoun σύ (sy, you) may be emphatically scornful: "You, a prisoner, deserted even by your friends, are a king, are you?" (Barrett 1978: 536).

"King of the Jews" may have been used by the Hasmoneans, who ruled Judea prior to the Roman subjugation of Palestine. The title is also applied to Herod the Great (Josephus, Ant. 16.10.2 §311). Pilate's question seeks to determine whether or not Jesus constituted a political threat to Roman imperial power (Bammel 1984: 417–19). His gubernatorial tenure was punctuated by outbursts of ethnic nationalism that rendered him ever more alert to potential sources of trouble, especially since Judea was "infested with brigands" (Ant. 20.9.5 §215) and "anyone might make himself king as the head of a band of rebels" (Ant. 17.10.8 §285 (Jensen 1941: esp. 261–62).

Jesus' response in 18:34–37 is more extensive than that recorded in the Synoptics (Ridderbos 1997: 593). His initial counterquestion draws attention away from himself to the Jews who had lodged their charges against him and possibly shows awareness of Pilate's disgust at having to interfere in internal Jewish matters. Jesus is fully aware that the epithet "king of the Jews" is capable of more than one definition, especially given the different cultural, political, and religious backgrounds of Jews and Romans. Hence, he cannot simply answer Pilate's question; he must first define the sense in which he is and is not a king.35

Pilate's riposte "Am I a Jew?" reveals the depth of his exasperation (Witherington 1995: 291). He realizes that he is getting drawn more and more deeply into a Jewish internecine dispute without being able to extricate himself. Moreover, though Pilate harbors contempt and resentment toward the Jews, ironically, he will be forced in the course of the investigation to adopt their position (Carson 1991: 593).

18:36–37 "My kingdom is not of this world. . . . But now my kingdom is not from here." Earlier, Jesus had rebuffed people's efforts to make him king (6:15). Apart from 3:3 and 3:5, this is the only instance of "kingdom" terminology in this Gospel, which stands in stark contrast with the Synoptics, where the phrase "kingdom of God" is exceedingly common. In both cases in the present Gospel, the use of the term seems to be constrained by the specific encounters of Jesus with Nicodemus and with Pilate and their notions, respectively, of a Jewish kingdom or the Roman Empire. In John, Jesus consistently disavows all political aspirations.

If Jesus were seeking political rule, his servants would fight to prevent his arrest by the Jews.39 Jesus here makes no mention of Peter's earlier efforts (recorded in 18:10–11) to do just that. Yet although Jesus disavows any political aspirations, he does not deny being a king. If he did, he would fail to testify to the truth. The phrase "I was born" constitutes the sole reference to Jesus' birth in this Gospel (Carson 1991: 594–95; Barrett 1978: 537). "Bear witness to the truth" harks back to similar language used earlier regarding John the Baptist (5:33).

When Jesus says, "Everyone on the side of truth listens to me," he makes Pilate palpably uncomfortable (see commentary at 18:38). For in truth, it is not Jesus who is on trial but rather Pilate, who is confronted with the "light of the world" and must decide whether he prefers darkness or light (R. Brown 1970: 868). Yet although Jesus' disavowal of an earthly kingship could have been reassuring for Pilate in that Jesus obviously was no threat to Roman hegemony, the procurator finds himself challenged to accept or reject the truth that Jesus has come to reveal (R. Brown 1970: 869; cf. Michaels 1989: 316).

18:38–40 "What is truth?" With this flippant remark, Pilate dismisses Jesus' claim that he came to testify to the truth and that everyone on the side of truth listens to him.

Rather than being philosophical in nature, Pilate's comment may reflect disillusionment (if not bitterness) from a political, pragmatic point of view. In his seven years as governor of Judea, he had frequently clashed with the Jewish population. And recently, his position with the Roman emperor had become increasingly tenuous (see commentary at 18:29).

After this, Pilate went out again to the Jews, returning to the outer colonnade (cf. 18:28–29). His statement "I find no basis for a charge against him" (cf. Luke 23:4, 14) indicates that he did not perceive Jesus as a rival aspirant to political office. At the same time, Pilate's thrice-repeated exoneration of Jesus (cf. John 19:4, 6) stands in blatant contrast with the actual death sentence pronounced in deference to the Jewish authorities.

"It is your custom for me to release to you one prisoner at the time of the Passover" (more literally, "at Passover"). There is little extrabiblical evidence for the custom of releasing one prisoner at Passover. The release probably served as a gesture of goodwill designed to lessen political antagonism and to assure people that "no one coming to Jerusalem would be caught in the midst of political strife."43 Roman law provided for two kinds of amnesty: pardoning a condemned criminal (indulgentia) and acquitting someone prior to the verdict (abolitio); in Jesus' case, the latter would have been in view (Keener 1993: 309).

The term "king of the Jews" in Pilate's mouth is used in a

mocking, derogatory sense (cf. 19:14, 15, 19–20), "expressing what he regards as the absurd nature of the charge made by the Jews" (Ridderbos 1997: 597–98). The strong word "shout" (κραυγάζω, kraugazō) is consistently used by John to describe the escalating dynamic of the mob's demands for Jesus' crucifixion. They then demanded, "No, not him! Give us Barabbas!"45 Generally, Zealot-style political extremism was condemned. Yet here the Jews, at the instigation of the high priests, ask for the release of Barabbas, a terrorist, while calling for the death of Jesus of Nazareth, who renounces all political aspirations (6:15; 18:36–37; see Burge 2000: 502). Apart from the irony of making such a person out to be a political threat, this demonstrates both the influence that the Sanhedrin had over the Jewish people at large and the Jewish authorities' determination to have Jesus executed in order to preserve their own privileged position (11:49–52; see also Acts 17:7).

Nothing is known of Barabbas apart from the Gospel evidence. He is called a λ῾στής lit., "one who seizes plunder"), which probably means not merely "robber" but "insurrectionist" (cf. Mark 15:7). Luke (23:19) indicates that Barabbas "had been thrown into prison for an insurrection in the city, and for murder." In Matt. 27:16, Barabbas is characterized as "notorious" (ἐπίσημος, episēmos). The irony is plain: the crowd prefers someone who had a track record of political subversiveness over someone who had no such record but who, to the contrary, had refused to define his mission primarily in political terms and who hardly represented a threat to the Roman

Empire (Duke 1985: 131).

b. Jesus Sentenced to Be Crucified (19:1–16a)

19:1–3   After the Jewish phase of the trial and Jesus' interrogation by Pilate, the sentencing stage begins. The day is April 3, A.D. 33, and Jesus' execution is imminent. Despite the governor's own personal conclusion that Jesus is innocent, he yields to Jewish demands for Jesus' crucifixion. The preferred Roman capital punishment for non-Roman citizens, crucifixion, is one of the most cruel and tortuous forms of death ever invented and inflicted in human history.

Pilate had Jesus flogged. From least to most severe, there were three forms of flogging administered by the Romans: (1) the fustigatio, a beating given for smaller offenses such as hooliganism, often accompanied by a severe warning; (2) the flagellatio, a more brutal flogging to which criminals were subjected whose offenses were more serious; and (3) the verberatio, the most terrible form of this punishment, regularly associated with other reprisals such as crucifixion.

In the present instance, the flogging probably in view is the least severe form, the fustigatio, which was intended in part to appease the Jews and in part to teach Jesus a lesson. After the sentence of crucifixion, Jesus was scourged again, this time in the most severe form, the verberatio. This explains why Jesus was too weak to carry his own cross very far (see commentary at 19:17). Also, the nearness of

The Passion of the Christ, 183

the special Sabbath meant that the agony of crucifixion must be kept short in order not to interfere with religious festivities (19:31–33).

Apparently, the "crown of thorns" consisted of some branches twisted together from the long spikes of the date palm, shaped into a mock "crown," the radiant corona, which adorns rulers' heads on many coins of Jesus' time (Bonner 1953). The thorns may have come from the common thorn bush (Isa. 34:13; Nah. 1:10) or from date palms that have thorns near the base. These thorns, which could be up to twelve inches long, would sink into the victim's skull, resulting in considerable pain. It is reasonable to surmise that onlookers would observe profuse bleeding and distortion of facial features.

The purple robe, probably a military cloak, was used as a mock royal garment (Carson 1984: 573). The Matthean parallel (27:28) refers to a "scarlet robe," a red chlamys or outer cloak worn by emperor, minor officials, and soldiers alike. John uses the term ἱμάτιον (himation) which denotes a person's "outer clothing" or "robe." Like Mark (15:17), John gives the robe's color as purple, the imperial color (1 Macc. 8:14); yet in the Book of Revelation, "purple and scarlet" are mentioned side by side (Rev. 17:4; 18:16). Because purple dye (taken from shellfish) was expensive, a genuine purple cloak was not as easily obtained as a red one. On the whole, ancient nomenclature of color appears to have been somewhat fluid.

"Hail, king of the Jews!" The soldiers' greeting mimics the

"Ave Caesar" extended to the Roman emperor. Their mocking of Jesus as king seems to copy scenes frequently featured on stage and in Roman circuses (Winter 1974: 148–49). The game of "mock king," scratchings of which are preserved on the stone pavement of the fortress of Antonia (see commentary at 19:13), was played by soldiers during the Roman Saturnalia. On the word for "slap in the face" or "blow" (ῥάπισμα, rhapisma), see commentary at 18:22. The imperfect ἐδίδοσαν (edidosan, they were giving) indicates repeated blows to the face (Schlatter 1948: 343). Matthew and Mark record the soldiers hitting Jesus on the head with a staff used as a mock scepter (Matt. 27:30 par.).

19:4–7 The scourging and the mockery of Jesus are part of Pilate's plan to convince the Jews of the absurdity of their accusation against Jesus (Ridderbos 1997: 600). The statement "I find no basis for a charge against him" reiterates 18:38. Usually, this "not guilty" verdict reached by the Roman governor would stand (especially if repeated three times [see 19:6]). But the Jewish leadership is not to be deterred.

"Here is the man!" "Man" may hark back to OT messianic passages such as Zech. 6:12 (Meeks 1967: 70–71). In classical literature the expression occasionally means "the poor fellow," "the poor creature." To be sure, in his mock regal garments, Jesus must have been a heartrending sight (Ridderbos 1997: 600; Carson 1991: 598). In John's context, Pilate's statement may also accentuate Jesus' humanity: Jesus is "the man," the God-sent Son of Man.

But similar to Pilate's attempt to release Jesus as part of a Passover custom, so also this attempt to sidestep his judicial authority failed (Ridderbos 1997: 601). The chief priests (see commentary at 7:32) called all the louder for Jesus' crucifixion. For the third and final time, Pilate asserts, "I find no basis for a charge against him" (19:6; cf. 18:38; 19:4). In first saying, "You take him and crucify him," Pilate uses sarcasm: he knows full well that the Jews do not have the authority to impose the death penalty, and if they did, they would stone rather than crucify Jesus (see commentary at 18:31).

"We have a law, and according to that law he must die, because he claimed to be the Son of God." A Roman prefect was responsible both for keeping peace and for maintaining local law. Jesus has frequently been accused of blasphemy (5:18; 8:59; 10:31, 33); yet in both the OT and other Jewish literature, the claim of being God's son need not be blasphemous and may refer to the anointed king of Israel (2 Sam. 7:14; Ps. 2:7; 89:26–27) or to the Messiah (4QFlor; see commentary at 1:49; Michel, NIDNTT 3:637).64

19:8–11 "Now when Pilate heard this statement, he grew even more afraid." Though Roman officials may have been cynical, they also were often deeply superstitious. In pagan ears, the designation "son of god" conjured up notions of "divine men," persons believed to enjoy certain divine powers.66 Ancient pagans concluded commonly enough that "the gods have come down to us in human form" (Acts 14:11). If Jesus was a "son of god," Pilate may have reasoned, he might incur the wrath of the gods for having Jesus flogged (cf. Matt. 27:19).

Alternatively, the root of Pilate's apprehension may have been political. He may have feared that the Jewish leaders would report to Rome that he failed to respect local religious customs, which was an accepted principle of provincial administration. This depiction of Pilate hardly fits with Josephus's portrayal of the early years of the Roman governor's tenure, where he ruthlessly broke up riots and stubbornly resisted Jewish demands. Yet it fits perfectly with Pilate's tenuous position subsequent to the execution of his mentor Aelius Sejanus in A.D. 31.

Pilate seeks to assuage the fear welling up inside by asking Jesus, "Where do you come from?" The question is profound, but once again Pilate is in no position to comprehend the truth regarding Jesus (cf. 18:38). In a parallel recorded by Josephus, the Roman procurator Albinus summons the prophet Jesus, son of Ananias, who had proclaimed the destruction of Jerusalem and the temple, inquiring who he is and where he comes from (J.W. 6.5.3 §305). During the course of Jesus' ministry, his origins frequently had been at issue in his dealings with his opponents (e.g., 7:27–28; 8:14; 9:29–30). On a literal level, Jesus' Galilean provenance places him under Herod Antipas's jurisdiction (cf. Luke 23:6–7). In the Johannine context, however, there are clearly spiritual overtones as well (18:36–37).

Jesus gave Pilate no answer. He and Pilate occupy entirely

different worlds, and no answer, short or long, would have been sufficient to adequately address Pilate's question (Carson 1991: 600). Jesus' silence also brings to mind the suffering Servant of Isaiah (53:7; cf. 1 Pet. 2:22–23). If Nicodemus and the Jewish authorities could not understand where Jesus had come from, how could this Roman governor be expected to grasp his true origin? The Greco-Roman pantheon was replete with gods having sexual union with women resulting in human offspring; a mind saturated with such myths would have grave difficulty comprehending Jesus' relationship with his Father. Jesus' silence obviously had an irritating effect on Pilate (cf. 19:10).

In issuing what Pilate must have known was a somewhat hollow threat in light of the Jews' leverage over him (Whitacre 1999: 450–51), he reminded Jesus, "I have power" (see commentary at 18:31; 19:6). Jesus' response is "typical of biblical compatibilism, even the worst evil cannot escape the outer boundaries of God's sovereignty—yet God's sovereignty never mitigates the responsibility and guilt of moral agents who operate under divine sovereignty, while their voluntary decisions and their evil rebellion never render God utterly contingent" (Carson 1991: 600).

Pilate finds himself in charge ultimately only because of God's sovereign action (Carson 1991: 601; Kruse 2003: 363, citing Dan. 2:20–21; 4:25). The Roman procurator is responsible for failing to act to preserve truth and justice, but "he did not initiate the trial or engineer the betrayal"

(Carson 1991: 602). In good Jewish manner, Jesus here uses "from above" as a circumlocution for God. As to the identity of "the one who handed me over to you," Judas is a possible candidate (6:71; 13:21; 18:2), but the more likely person is Caiaphas (18:30, 35; cf. 11:49–53; Mark 14:61–64), since Judas drifts from view subsequent to Jesus' arrest in 18:12.

19:12 From then on, Pilate tried to set Jesus free. Apparently, Pilate remained unconvinced of Jesus' guilt (cf. 18:38; 19:4, 6). "Neither the charge of sedition nor the additional charge of blasphemy held up in Pilate's eyes" (Carson 1991: 602). Perhaps also owing to his superstitious nature (19:8) and because he was impressed by Jesus' courage in the face of death (considered virtuous in the Greco-Roman world), he was reluctant to have Jesus crucified. Yet as in other instances, Pilate, despite his boast to Jesus that he had power to release and power to crucify (19:10; see R. Brown 1970: 894), would eventually yield to Jewish demands (see Philo, Gaius 38 §§301–2).

Pilate had reason to fear the threat of the Jewish leaders—they had conveyed their displeasure with Pilate to the emperor on earlier occasions—for Tiberius was known to act decisively when suspicions were cast on the conduct or loyalty of his subordinates. By the time of Vespasian (A.D. 69–71), "friend of Caesar" had become virtually an official title; even in Jesus' day, the term may have had semitechnical force. It is possible that Pilate had acquired "friend of Caesar" status through his mentor Sejanus.[76] But since Sejanus recently had fallen from grace (executed

October 18, A.D. 31), Pilate would have ample reason to be concerned that his favored status with the emperor likewise would be removed.

19:13 After several futile attempts to elude the Jews' grasp, Pilate finally sits down on his judgment seat to render "his judicial decision on the one who alone is the promised Messiah, the one to whom the Father himself entrusted all (eschatological) judgment (5:22)" (Carson 1991: 603). The β?μα (bēma, judge's seat), or sella curilis, normally stood in the forecourt of the governor's residence. It was elevated, so the judge could look out over the spectators. Matthew depicts the entire trial with Pilate seated on the judge's seat and Jesus standing before him.
The Greek term λιθόστρωτον (lithostr?ton) may refer to different kinds of stone pavement, ranging from simple ones consisting of identical pieces to elaborate ones of fine mosaic. In light of the pavement's location in front of the governor's residence, where traffic would have been heavy, a simple pavement of large stones is most likely. The meaning of "Gabath" (cf. Gibeah, birthplace of Saul [1 Sam. 11:4]) is given as "hill" by the Jewish historian Josephus (J.W. 5.2.1 §51).

19:14 Some argue that παρασκευή (paraskeu?, Day of Preparation) refers to the day preceding Passover, that is, the day on which preparations for Passover are made (in the present case, Thursday morning). If so, then John indicates that Jesus is sent to be executed at the time at which Passover lambs are slaughtered in the temple. The Synoptists, however, clearly portray Jesus and his disciples as celebrating the Passover on the night prior to the crucifixion. Moreover, Matthew, Mark, Luke, and Josephus all use παρασκευή to refer to the day preceding the Sabbath. The term therefore should be taken to refer to the day of preparation for the Sabbath (i.e., Friday).83

If this is accurate, then το? πάσχα (tou pascha) means not "of the Passover," but "of Passover week." Indeed, "Passover" may refer to the (day of) the actual Passover meal or, as in the present case, the entire Passover week, including Passover day as well as the associated Feast of Unleavened Bread. "Day of Preparation of Passover week" is therefore best taken to refer to the day of preparation for the Sabbath (i.e., Friday) of Passover week (so, rightly, Carson 1991: 603–4; see also commentary at 19:31). Thus, all four Gospels concur that Jesus' last supper was a Passover meal eaten on Thursday evening (by Jewish reckoning, the onset of Friday).

For the time reference to "about the sixth hour," see commentary at 1:39. Reckoning time from dawn to dark, "sixth hour" would be about noon. Mark 15:25 indicates that Jesus' crucifixion took place at the "third hour," that is, about 9:00 A.M. But since people related the estimated time to the closest three-hour mark, any time between 9:00 A.M. and noon may have led one person to say that an event occurred at the third (9:00 A.M.) or the sixth hour (12:00 noon) (Blomberg 1987: 180; Morris 1995: 708). Mark's concern likely was to provide the setting for the three hours of darkness (15:25, 33), while John seeks to stress the length of the proceedings, starting in the "early morning" (18:28) before Pilate.

"Here is your king." Once again, Pilate caustically presents the Jews with "their king," mocking their implicit contention that "even the emperor in Rome has to be on his guard" in light of Jesus' claims (Ridderbos 1997: 606). By his sarcastic "acclamation," Pilate "simultaneously throws up with bitter irony the spurious charge of sedition in their face, and mocks their vassal status by saying that this bloodied and helpless prisoner is the only king they are likely to have" (Carson 1991: 605). Yet, like Caiaphas earlier (11:49–52), Pilate spoke better than he knew. Jesus was indeed the "king of the Jews," the king of Israel (1:49), as John had come to believe, and the present travesty of justice is part of God's paradoxical plan of reversal by which the world's judgment is confounded by God's judgment of sin in Christ.

19:15   At this the members of the Sanhedrin strike the exceedingly "cynical pose … of loyal subjects of the emperor" (Ridderbos 1997: 606): "We have no king but Caesar!" The OT frequently reiterates that Yahweh alone is the true king of Israel (e.g., Judg. 8:23; 1 Sam. 8:7). None of the foreign overlords qualified, whether Persian, Greek, or Roman (cf. Isa. 26:13). The very Feast of Passover, which the Jews are in the process of celebrating, is built on God's unique and supreme role in the life of the nation. The eleventh of the ancient Eighteen Benedictions prays, "Reign over us, you alone."

Yet here, by professing to acknowledge Caesar alone as their king, the Jewish leaders betray their entire national heritage, as well as deny their own messianic expectations based on the promises of Scripture (Beasley-Murray 1999: 343). This, then, is the Fourth Evangelist's point, especially for his first Jewish readers: the Jewish rejection of the Messiah involved religious compromise and a failure to worship God. Yet the Jews, too, spoke better than they knew. For in truth, the Jews joined the world in its rejection of the God-sent Messiah, thus failing to give homage to God and showing that they had, in fact, no king but Caesar (Morris 1995: 710).

19:16a At that point Pilate handed Jesus over to "them" to be crucified, whereby "them" presumably refers in the immediate instance to the soldiers, but secondarily also indicates that Pilate handed Jesus over in order to satisfy the Jews. The usual form of death sentence was Ibis in crucem, "On the cross you shall go" (Petronius, Satyricon 137). Upon pronouncement of the sentence, the criminal was first scourged, then executed (Josephus, J.W. 2.14.9 §308).

4. Jesus' Crucifixion and B

Kostenberger, A. J. (2004). John. Baker exegetical commentary on the New Testament (510–540). Grand Rapids, Mich.: Baker Academic.

According to the Feast Schedule GOD gave Moses in Exodus 12 On the 10th day of the month the Passover lamb was chosen by the High priest from the sheepfolds in Bethlehem and then paraded through Jerusalem to the cheers and waving of Branches of the pilgrims there for the

Feast. A lamb was also chosen for each household.

Jesus Christ, the Passover Lamb, was born in Bethlehem and entered the Jerusalem triumphantly on the foal of a donkey to the praise of Psalm 118 and waving of palm frawns fulfilling the Prophesy from Zechariah 9:9 and Micah 5:2 .

GOD asked Abraham to sacrifice his son, The Son whom he loved. When Abraham took Isaac up on mount Moriah and laid him on the altar and raised the knife to kill his son the angel of the Lord stopped Abraham and it was considered accomplished and Isaac questioned "Where is the lamb" Gen 22:8 And Abraham said, "My son, God will provide for Himself the lamb for the burnt offering." Don't be confused by the ram caught in the bush that Abraham and Isaac sacrifice, the lamb sacrifice The Father provided for Himself was Jesus Christ.

The next instruction from GOD for His Feast (Ex 12) was to care for the lamb until the fourteenth day of the month when each family would kill the Passover lamb at Twilight and eat it with bitter herbs and unleavened bread.

Jesus was in the Temple at Passover year 27 AD
John 2:19 Yeshua answered them, "Destroy this temple, and in three days I will raise it up again."
John 2:20 The Judeans said, "It took 46 years to build this Temple, and you're going to raise it in three days?" John 2:21 But the "temple" he had spoken of was his body.

The Passion of the Christ, 194

The Temple was started to be rebuilt in 19 BC. 46 years minus 19 years = year 27.
One year later Jesus would be crucified at Passover and raised on the third day, in 28 AD.

Jesus was about thirty when he was Baptized Luke 3:23

If you believe that we have such a High Priest. Scripture tells us, (Hebrews 8:1-11) the answer to those Jewish people who taunted the early Christians with the words, "We have the tabernacle; we have the priesthood; we have the offerings; we have the ceremonies; we have the temple; we have the beautiful priestly garments." The believers' in Jesus as the Messiah answer is, "Yes, you have the shadows but we have the fulfillment. You have the ceremonies but we have Christ. You have the pictures but we have the Person. And our High Priest is seated at the right hand of the throne of the Majesty in the heavens. No other high priest ever sat down in recognition of a finished work, and none ever held such a place of honor and power." There were no chairs in the Temple for sitting and the Priesthood was not allowed to sit, that is the important point to our High Priest sitting at the right hand of GOD.

Counting Backward from the Resurrection,
which is prior to Mary's arrival at the tomb,
before first light, on the first day of the week.

Using the Arrival at the Tomb, on the first day of the week, before light or at Dawn, and finding the Tomb empty as the ending event confirmed by all four Gospels, the timeline in

The Passion of the Christ, 195

reverse would be as follows:

18th day of the month, First day of the week, Day of the First Fruits offering

17th day of the month (Sabbath), Resurrection at the end of the day (3rd night and day)

16th day of the month 2nd night and day in the Tomb

15th day of the month High Sabbath of Unleavened Bread and 1st night and day in the Tomb

14th day of the month Passover Death from Crucifixion at twilight

13th day of the month Last Supper at the ending of the 4th and last day of preparation

12th day of the month Third day of Feast Preparation

11th day of the month Second day of Feast Preparation

10th day of the month (Sabbath) Triumphal Entry and choosing of the Passover Lamb

9th day of the month 6th day of the week

8th day of Nisan (Abib) Jesus arrival in Bethany 6 days before Passover

This Calendar is built from the last event to arrival in Bethany six days prior to Passover and shows the progression of events according to the requirements of the Feasts of GOD.

Also by the Author

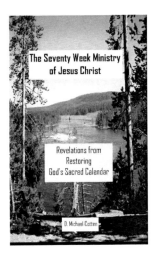

The Seventy Week Ministry of Jesus Christ: Revelations from Restoring God's Sacred Calendar

by Michael Cotten
ISBN: 978-0982480274
260 pages
$15.99

You're Not Special Because You Love God . . . You're Special Because God Loves You!

by Michael Cotten
ISBN: 978-1936497034
110 pages
$14.99

Printed by BoD™in Norderstedt, Ge

9 781936 497195